£1.70

ALIVE

7-19-90
7/28/03 - C

BC

...IANS

...rlow

Sussex, England ~~~~

EVERYDAY PUBLICATIONS

230 GLEBEMOUNT AVENUE
TORONTO, CANADA, M4C 3T4

THE KING'S INSTITUTE
THE CHURCH ON THE WAY

International Standard Book Number: 0-919586-12-0

Copyright © 1972
by R.E. Harlow

Second edition, 1975
Third edition, 1977

Cover design by Michael Landgraff

Printed in Canada

ALIVE AND FREE

Paul wrote many letters to Christians and Christian churches. The Holy Spirit led him to write 13 letters which are in the New Testament, and perhaps the letter to the Hebrews also. All books in the Bible are true, but the letters of Paul contain the most wonderful truths in the Scripture. We should study them very carefully and ask the Lord to help us to understand.

* * * * * * *

In Romans the Holy Spirit shows us that we are ALIVE and FREE - in Christ Jesus. God gives us life forever and we can live for Him day by day, 6.23; 14.8. He makes us free from sin because the Lord Jesus paid the whole debt and the Spirit gives us power to live a holy life, 6.22. This is the Good News explained in Romans: **in Christ you can be alive and free.**

HOW TO READ THIS BOOK

The best way to read the Bible is to read a little every day. You can read through the book of Romans and this book about Romans in four months, if you follow the plan on page 5.

First you read a few verses in Romans, and then you read the paragraph which explains them. You will see on the next page which verses to read every day. On the first day of the month read Romans 1.1-3. On page 9 you will see a little 1/1 at the left. This shows you where you start reading in this book on the first day. On the second day read Romans 1.4-7 and read on pages 12 and 13 what is said about these verses beginning at 1/2.

This plan will help you to read through the book of Romans and this book in four months. You can start any month. Write in the name of the month at the top of page 5. If you want to start before the first day of the month, read a little every day, then start over again on the first day of the month. If the month has already started, you could read every day the verses for two days until you catch up.

Some days you will see a question marked with square brackets. You will find the answer for these questions in the Bible in the verses given.

Some days there are no verses to read but questions to answer. There are questions after each chapter of the book of Romans; these are to help you test yourself. You should answer these questions and then look up the answers on pages 137-144. We hope that you will understand everything and that the Lord will give you blessing and real joy as you read it.

READ THE BIBLE EVERY DAY

DAY	FIRST MONTH	SECOND MONTH	THIRD MONTH	FOURTH MONTH
1	1. 1— 3	TEST	8.38,39	12.14—16
2	1. 4— 7	5. 1— 5	TEST	12.17—21
3	1. 8—12	5. 6— 8	9. 1— 5	TEST
4	1.13—15	5. 9—11	9. 6— 9	13. 1— 5
5	1.16,17	5.12—17	9.10—13	13. 6,7
6	1.18—20	5.18—21	9.14—18	13. 8—10
7	1.21—23	TEST	9.19—21	13.11—14
8	1.24—27	6. 1, 2	9.22—26	TEST
9	1.28—32	6' 3— 6	9.27—29	14. 1— 4
10	TEST	6. 7—11	9.30—33	14. 5— 9
11	2. 1— 4	6.12—14	TEST	14.10—12
12	2. 5—11	6.15—19	10. 1— 4	14.13—18
13	2.12—16	6.20—23	10. 5— 9	14.19—23
14	2.17—24	TEST	10.10—13	TEST
15	2.25—29	7. 1— 3	10.14—17	15. 1— 6
16	TEST	7. 4— 6	10.18—21	15. 7,8
17	3. 1— 4	7. 7—11	TEST	15. 9—13
18	3. 5— 8	7.12,13	11. 1— 6	15.14—16
19	3. 9—18	7.14—20	11. 7—10	15.17—21
20	3.19, 20	7.21—25	11.11—15	15.22—24
21	3.21—24	TEST	11.16—18	15.25—29
22	3.25, 26	8. 1— 4	11.19—21	15.30—33
23	3.27—31	8. 5— 8	11.22—24	TEST
24	TEST	8. 9—13	11.25—29	16. 1, 2
25	4. 1— 5	8.14—17	11.30—32	16. 3— 7
26	4. 6— 8	8.18—22	11.33—36	16. 8—11
27	4. 9—12	8.23—25	TEST	16.12—16
28	4.13—15	8.26—30	12. 1, 2	16.17—20
29	4.16—21	8.31—34	12. 3— 8	16.21—24
30	4.22—25	8.35—37	12. 9—13	16.25—27

THE BOOK OF ROMANS

1. GOD HAS REVEALED THE GOOD NEWS, 1.1-17
   Paul greeted the Christians at Rome, 1.1-7
   Paul wanted to visit the believers at Rome, 1.8-15
   Paul explained why the Good News is so important, 1.16,17

2. GOD WILL JUDGE ALL MEN, 1.18 - 3.20
God will judge the Gentiles, 1.18-32
God will judge good men, 2.1-16
   Those who judge, 2.1-11
   God will judge all men fairly, 2.12-16
God will judge the Jews, 2.17-29
   The Jews are also guilty, 2.17-24
   What should the Jews really be like? 2.25-29
God will judge all men, 3.1-20

3. GOD CAN SAVE MEN FROM THEIR SINS, 3.21 - 5.21
   God forgives men's sins if they believe, 3.21 - 4.25
      God justifies men, 3.21-31
      The story of Abraham, chapter 4
         Abraham was justified by faith, 4.1-8
         Paul explains these truths more fully, 4.9-25
   God gives many other blessings to those who believe, 5.1-11
   Christ is like Adam, but far greater, 5.12-21

4. GOD CAN KEEP US FROM SINNING, chapters 6 - 8
   Christ delivered us from sin, chapter 6
      Alive to God, 6.1-11
      Servants of God, 6.12-23
   The Lord delivers us from the law, chapter 7
      How long can law make a claim over men? 7.1-6
      Why did God give the law? 7.7-11
      The law is good, 7.12-13
      Why is the law weak? 7.14-20
      God can deliver us from our own weakness, 7.21-25

6. GOD WANTS US TO LIVE A HOLY LIFE, chapters 12 - 15

How we should act toward God and men, chapter 12
We should know and do the will of God, 12.1,2
We should help other Christians, 12.3-13
In the assembly, 12.3-8
Love and joy, 12.9-13
We should be kind to all men, 12.14-21

How we should act in relation to the world, chapter 13
Obey the government, 13.1-7
Love your neighbour, 13.8-14

A weak brother, 14.1 - 15.6
Who is a weak brother? 14.1-5
The weak brother and the Lord, 14.6-12
Strong and weak brothers, 14.13-23
Help one another, 15.1-6

Our relation to all men, 15.7-33
Receive all true believers, 15.7
The Jews should have taught men about God, 15.8-13
The Lord commanded Paul to preach to the Gentiles, 15.14-33
Paul's methods, 15.14-21
Paul's plans, 15.22-29
Paul asked the Christians to pray for him, 15.30-33

7. GOD HONOURS HIS PEOPLE WHO SERVE HIM, chapter 16

Paul recommended Phoebe, 16.1,2

Paul's friends in Rome, 16.3-16

Do not receive trouble makers, 16.17-20

Several people in Corinth sent their greetings to the believers in Rome, 16.21-24

Praise to God, 16.25-27

ALIVE AND FREE

STUDIES IN ROMANS

Paul's letter to the Christians at Rome is one of the most important books in the Bible. The Holy Spirit told Paul what to write and we can learn a great deal about God and how to be saved in this letter. The book of Romans has seven parts:

1. God has revealed the Good News, 1.1-17.
2. God will judge all men, 1.18 - 3.20.
3. God can save men from their sins, 3.21 - 5.21.
4. God can keep us from sinning, chapters 6 - 8.
5. God has His plans for Israel, chapters 9 - 11.
6. God wants us to live a holy life, chapters 12 - 15.
7. God honours His people who serve Him, chapter 16.

We will study every verse in all 16 chapters of Romans; let us ask the Lord to help us really to understand.

GOD HAS REVEALED
THE GOOD NEWS
1.1-17

1. GOD HAS REVEALED THE GOOD NEWS. 1.1-17

1/1 *The first part of Romans tells us what Paul's whole letter is about: the* **Good News.** *This Good News reveals the Lord Jesus Christ and tells us about Him. Paul knew that this message was*

God's way to save men and he was not ashamed of it. This first part of Romans has three sections:

1. *Paul greeted the Christians at Rome, vs.1-7.*
2. *He wanted to visit them, vs.8-15.*
3. *The Good News is important, vs.16,17.*

Paul greeted the Christians at Rome, 1.1-7

1. Who was Paul? He called himself a servant of Christ Jesus and an apostle. Paul was born in a Jewish family which belonged to the tribe of Benjamin. He grew up in the city of Tarsus, but travelled a long distance to Jerusalem to study the Old Testament under a famous teacher, Gamaliel. Paul was a good student and became very zealous for the law, Philippians 3.5,6. He heard about the Lord Jesus, but at first he did not believe in Him, Acts 7.58. In fact he tried to stop others from following the Lord, Acts 8.3. Until that day on the road to Damascus! There the Lord Jesus spoke to Paul and he accepted Him as his Lord and Saviour, Acts 9.1-6. Then Paul became a very faithful servant of Christ, Galatians 1.10; Titus 1.1.

[Other men also were *servants* or slaves of the Lord Jesus Christ. Write down the names of seven servants:

Philippians 1.1 _____   Colossians 1.7 _____
Colossians 4.7 _____   James 1.1 _____
2 Peter 1.1 _____   Jude verse 1 _____
Revelation 1.1_____]

We are all servants of Christ Jesus, Romans 12.11; 1 Peter 2.16, and we must obey Him as our Lord, but there are no true apostles today. The Lord Jesus chose twelve apostles, but one of them betrayed Him to His enemies and then killed himself. Peter and the other disciples chose Matthias to take Judas' place, Acts 1.26. Paul and Barnabas are called apostles, Acts 14.4; also Silas and Timothy, 1 Thessalonians 1.1; 2.6.

All these men died long ago. Many of them wrote parts of the New Testament.

[Write down the names of the apostles who were led by the Holy Spirit to write one book or more of the New Testament. Do not include James because the man who wrote this letter was not an apostle._____
————————————————————————————]

Today we cannot ask the apostles to tell us what God wants us to do, but we can read what the apostles wrote in the New Testament. This will show us God's will.

The word apostle also means *messenger.* For example, Titus and Epaphroditus were messengers of churches, 2 Corinthians 8.23; Philippians 2.25. The Lord Jesus has sent us as His messengers to the world, John 20.21; Romans 10.15.

God called Paul to be an apostle and set him apart to preach the *Good News,* v.1; Galatians 1.15; Acts 13.2. What is the Good News? The next few verses tell us about the Good News.

The word *Gospel* or Good News is used twelve more times in Romans: 1.9,15,16; 2.16; 10.15,16; 11.28; 15.16,19,20,29; 16.25.

---

2. Long ago God promised men that He would send a Saviour to deliver them from the power of Satan, Genesis 3.15. Many other verses in the Old Testament tell us about the coming Saviour and King. Some of the writers of the Old Testament are called *prophets;* they spoke for God, and the Holy Spirit often told them about future events. The Old Testament is the Word of God, so Paul called it the *Holy Scriptures.*

3. The Good News tells about God's Son. The Lord Jesus Christ is a Descendant of King David, and we can read the names of His ancestors in Luke 3.23-38. The Lord Jesus was a Man, the Perfect Man. He is also the Son of God.

Christ was shown to be the Son of God:
Old Testament prophets said the Saviour would come, v.2;
New Testament writers show He is the Descendant
    of David, v.3;
He lived a holy life, the only Perfect Man, v.4;
He had power to do many miracles, v.4;
God raised Him from the dead, v.4.

1/2   **4.** The Lord Jesus lived a perfectly holy life in this world; this proved that He is God's Son. God showed that Christ was His Son by giving Him authority to do great miracles, John 5.36. The Lord Jesus raised three persons from death: a man, a young man, and a girl, John 11.43,44; Luke 7.14,15; Mark 5.35-42. God gave part of the Spirit's power to a few men, but **fully** to the Lord Jesus Christ, John 3.34. Still men refused the Saviour and nailed Him on a cross. God raised Him from death and showed to all that the Lord Jesus is His Son.

Some people think that God could not have a son unless He had a wife, but this is a mistake. God did not create His Son: the Son is eternal. He had no beginning and He will never have an end, John 1.1; 17.5; Revelation 1.18. Other people teach that **all** men are sons of God. It is true that God created all people, but it is also true that all have sinned against Him. The Bible teaches that sinners can **become** sons of God if they believe in the Lord Jesus Christ, John 1.12. But the Lord Jesus never **became** the Son of God; He always was and always will be God the Son. The Bible calls us *sons of God,* 1 John 3.1,2, but Christ is the Son of God.

Christ, the Son of God

◄──────────────────────────────────────►

No beginning

No end

Men may become sons of God

Have a beginning - but no ending

5. So the Good News is about God's Son, and God chose Paul to take this message to all people. Those who hear this message should believe and obey. **6.** Some people in Rome heard and obeyed and believed, 9.24. **7.** Paul wrote this letter to them and told them that God loved them, called them and made them His own *saints.* Paul greeted them by praying that God would send them grace and peace from Himself and His Son.

The Bible calls all God's people *saints* because God has set us apart for Himself. In the Greek New Testament the same word is used for *saint* and *Holy* Scripture, v.2, and the *Holy* Spirit, 5.5. We should live holy lives as the Scripture teaches, because God has set us apart for Himself. The Holy Spirit will help us.

Paul also greeted other churches by asking God to send them *grace and peace*. He wrote nine letters to churches, in Rome, Corinth, Galatia, Ephesus, Philippi, Colossae and Thessalonica. He also wrote four other letters to Timothy (2), Titus and Philemon. In all of these letters he greeted the believers by asking God to send them grace and peace. In the two letters to Timothy he asked for grace, *mercy,* and peace. We believe that Paul also wrote to the Hebrews but that letter does not start off in the same way.

Where was Paul when he wrote this letter to the Romans? He did not say just where he was, but he was taking some money to the Christians at Jerusalem, money which had been given by the believers in Macedonia and Achaia which is now called Greece, 15.25, 26. Paul stayed in Greece for three months just before he went to Jerusalem, Acts 20.2,3; 21.17. It may well be that he wrote this letter at that time. [Look for these places on the map on page 15.]

Paul wanted to visit the believers at Rome, 1.8-15

1/3   Paul loved God's people who lived in Rome. **8.** First he thanked God for every one of them because they believed in the Lord. The news of their faith was spreading to people in all parts of the world. Rome was the greatest of all cities in those days and many people were talking about these believers who had turned to Christ and stopped worshipping idols. So people who did not believe in Christ were spreading the Good News.

Paul gave thanks to God *through* the Lord Jesus Christ. We should come to God through Christ at all times, both to pray and to worship Him, John 16.24; Hebrews 10.19.

9. If an honest man says something, it is probably true, and if two or three witnesses agree, most people will believe them, Deuteronomy 19.15; Matthew 18.16; 2 Corinthians 13.1. Here Paul told the Christians at Rome that **God** was his witness and not man. God knew that Paul was serving Him with his spirit and that he prayed for the believers at Rome. Paul remembered these people every time he prayed to God. **10.** He especially wanted to go to Rome to see the believers there, but he prayed for this **only** if it was God's will. Travelling was very dangerous in those days and Paul wanted to be sure that God was leading him to Rome. We will learn more of Paul's plans in 15.22-32.

> We should always ask God to lead us before we make any plans, James 4.13-15. He wants us to *worship* and *serve* Him with our spirit, John 4.24; Philippians 3.3. We serve God when we tell others the Good News about His Son, but we should first worship Him and thank Him for His love to us, Matthew 4.10.

11. Paul wanted to see these believers and to help them to be better Christians. He could teach them more about God's Word, and the Holy Spirit would give them spiritual gifts, 12.6-8; 1 Corinthians 12.8-10. This would make the church stronger and would comfort and encourage the people of God. **12.** Their faith would help Paul and his faith would help them.

1/4   **13.** Paul wanted the Roman Christians to know that he had often tried to visit them, Acts 19.21, but something happened every time to keep him from going to see them. He hoped that God would bless his service in Rome as He had done in other places. Paul preached the Good News from the time he first accepted Jesus Christ as his Lord, Acts 9.5,20. He had won people for Christ in Cyprus, Galatia, Macedonia, Greece and Asia Minor. He wanted to do the same at Rome.

Paul had started or planted many churches, but he had never been in Rome. Some people think that Peter started the church of Rome, but the Bible does not tell us that Peter was ever at Rome. Paul sent greetings to many believers in Rome, 16.3-16, but he did not even refer to Peter anywhere in this letter. Who started the church at Rome? We read that many visitors from Rome were at Jerusalem on the day of Pentecost when the Holy Spirit came on all the believers, Acts 2.10. They heard the Good News and some believed it. These people may have gone back to Rome and preached to others, both Jews and Gentiles. The Jewish Christians understood the Old Testament very well and Paul used over 60 verses from the Old Testament in this letter to the Romans. There were also many Gentile Christians in Rome.

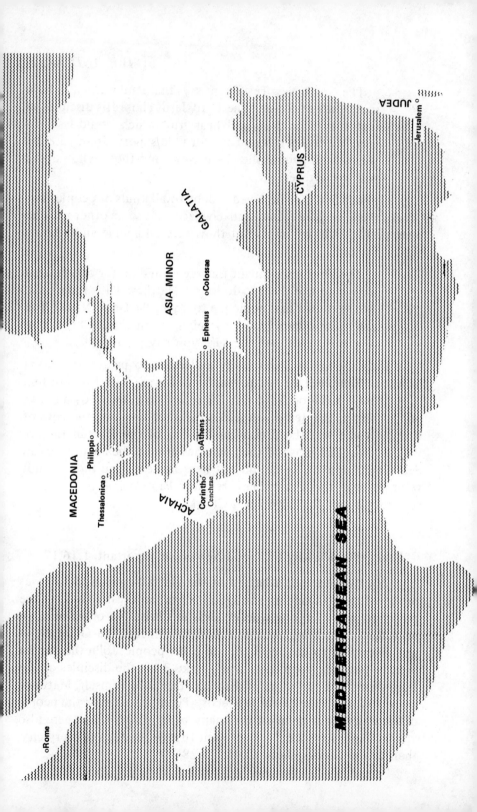

The Greek New Testament says that Paul wanted to have some *fruit* at Rome. The Lord Jesus chose His disciples so that they should go and bear fruit which would last forever. We too can bear fruit for God's glory, John 15.8,16. We can tell people the Good News and those who believe will live forever.

14. Paul felt that he owed a debt to all kinds of people. The Greeks were well educated and civilized, but some other nations were perhaps still ignorant. But they were all people and all men need a Saviour.

The Lord Jesus taught that we should do for others what we would like them to do for us, Matthew 7.12; Luke 6.31. Are you glad that someone told you the Good News? You can make others happy by telling them about Christ. You *owe* this to all men. Be sure you pay your debts.

15. Paul himself was ready and eager to preach the Good News at Rome, but he had to wait until it was God's time for him to go there. The Good News was the record of a Jew who had been put to death; the Jews had accused Him of breaking the laws of Rome. Rome was the proud capital city of the Roman Empire which controlled most of the countries around the Mediterranean Sea. The people of Rome did not like the Jews, and they did not want to hear about some new religion. Paul desired to tell them the truth about the Lord Jesus Christ.

Paul explained why the Good News is so important, 1.16,17

1/5   **16.** Paul was not ashamed of the Good News; in fact he was proud of it. No wonder. The Good News shows that God has the power to save everyone who believes in Christ. No other message or religion can bring such salvation to sinners. The Good News was given *first* to the Jews, then to other people. John the Baptist preached to the people of Israel, Luke 3.18; the disciples of the Lord Jesus did the same and so did the Lord Himself, Matthew 10.6; 15.24. On the day of Pentecost, Peter preached to the people of Jerusalem, but people from many other places were there also at that time, Acts 2.5,14. Paul went first to the Jews in every city, then to the Greeks, Acts 13.46; 28.28.

No one who believes in the Lord Jesus Christ will find out later that He has failed him, 9.33; 10.11. Paul suffered a great deal on his way to Rome and more still when he got there. Still he was never ashamed of the Lord Jesus, 2 Timothy 1.12.

We may well be ashamed of the sinful life we used to live, 6.21, but never of our Saviour. If we are, He will be ashamed of us, Mark 8.38.

17. The Good News tells us that God wants to be gracious to all men, Acts 20.24, but here the Good News shows that God is *righteous.* This word *righteous* or *just* is very common in the book of Romans, in fact, it is found 65 times. God is *righteous:* He must judge sin. He also "puts men right with Himself". This does not mean that these men have never sinned; we know that all are guilty. It means that the Lord Jesus Christ paid the debt and took our punishment and now God shows to all that we are free. The Holy Spirit teaches this wonderful truth very clearly in the first half of Romans. Here in verse 17 we learn only that the Good News reveals that God is righteous.

God is righteous. Is this a message of Good News to the sinner? No, because the righteous God must judge sin. And God cannot declare any man to be righteous just because he has done many good things. God can do this only because we have faith and believe in Christ. We had a little faith when we first trusted the Lord. We then started to learn more about Him and more about His Word. Our faith became greater and we grew from a little faith to more faith.

The *GOOD NEWS* shows	God's **power**, He is able to save
	1) Jews, v.16
	2) Gentiles,
	    educated, v.14
	    uneducated

The *GOOD NEWS* shows	God's **righteousness,** v.17

Then Paul used a verse from the Old Testament to prove this. The Old Testament is the book of God's law, and it teaches that any man who keeps God's commands will have life, Ezekiel 20.11. No one has ever been able to do this perfectly, but many men have faith and put their trust in God. So the Holy Spirit said that men of *faith* are righteous (or just) and they are the ones who will live.

You see, the sinner is guilty before God, the Judge of all the world, and he must die for his sins. The Bible says he is *dead* already: he does not have eternal life. God gives eternal life as a gift to all those who have faith, Ephesians 2.1-8. So men who are right with God through faith are the men who have life, eternal life. They get this life through faith and they continue to live by faith, Habakkuk 2.4. This truth is so important that the Holy Spirit repeats it three times in the New Testament: Romans 1.17; Galatians 3.11; Hebrews 10.38. Read these verses in Galatians and Hebrews, also a few verses before and after them.

The first part of Romans, 1.1-17, is quite short but extremely important. It shows that the Good News is about our Lord Jesus Christ, the Son of God and the Son of Man, who died and rose from death. The Good News tells that a sinner can get right with God if he has faith and believes in the Lord Jesus. This message is for all men, Jews and Gentiles, civilized and uneducated, in the whole world.

Read these 17 verses again and also the notes in this book which explain the meaning of the verses. If you understand these truths a little, you should thank the Lord for all He has done for you. You should also tell others about our wonderful Saviour.

GOD WILL JUDGE

ALL MEN

1.18 - 3.20

1/6   The second part of Romans teaches that God must judge all men because all have sinned. This is not Good News, but this part of Romans prepares us for the wonderful truths which are taught in the next part. The second part of Romans has four main sections:

1. The Gentiles, 1.18-32
2. Good men, 2.1-16
3. The Jews, 2.17-29
4. All men, 3.1-20

God will judge the Gentiles, 1.18-32

God called Abraham to leave his home and his family and go to the land of Canaan. He promised to make his descendants into a great nation and most of the Old Testament is about the nation of Israel. The people of Israel called all other nations **Gentiles**. God gave special privileges to Israel, but He loved all other people also. In the rest of this chapter we see that:

1. God has revealed Himself in the world of nature, vs.18-20.
2. Men have rejected God, vs.21-23, 25, 27, 28, 32.
3. God has rejected men, vs.24, 26, 28.

18. God is righteous and He hates sin. He becomes angry when men break His laws. For example, God sent a flood of water to destroy men in the days of Noah. He sent fire from heaven to punish the wicked men of Sodom and Gomorrah. He is angry with all kinds of sin which men commit. You say men do not know any

19

better? All men have a little truth but they do not follow it or do what is right. They *hold* the truth, but not in a righteous way. This is really holding *back* the truth which they should tell to other people. **19.** Men are able to know something about God and God has given all men some truth about Himself.

20. No man can see God, but all can see the world which He created. Anyone can look at the sun, moon and stars, the world of nature, and ask, "Who made it all?" The Maker of heaven and earth must have great power. The Bible tells us about God, but even people without the Bible can know two things:

1. God made the world;
2. He has great power.

No man can say he never had any opportunity to learn about God; no one has any excuse for not knowing God.

One day Paul was able to speak to some Gentile people in the city of Athens. He told them about the God in heaven who created the world and keeps everything going. He said that the men of Athens should seek for the true God and not worship images made of gold and silver and stone. You can read Paul's message in Acts 17.22-34.

1/7   **21.** The fact is, men **do** know God and they ought to honour Him. Instead, most people do not even thank God for the food they eat every day. They forget about God and leave Him out of their thoughts. Soon they cannot think clearly about any problem and their minds become dark. **22.** They think they are wise but God calls them *fools*. [What does God call the man who says there is no god? Psalm 14.1 .... What does God call the wisdom of this world? 1 Corinthians 1.20 ....] **23.** Men should worship God because He is eternal and never changes. Instead of that, men have made images of men and animals which must die; they worship these and forget the true God.

The Greeks made beautiful images of men and women and said, "These are our gods." The Egyptians made images of animals and things which fly or creep. Animals spend their lives seeking for food and pleasure. Men are greater than animals and should seek after God. God is greater than men and we should never fall down and worship the image of any creature, Exodus 20.3-6.

1/8   **24.** Men forget about God, so God *gives them up* and lets them do what they want. They do shameful things with each other which have a bad effect on their bodies. **25.** They go still further away from God. They refuse to believe the truth about God, so they begin to believe a lie instead. They worship and serve created things instead of God only, Matthew 4.10. Some try to worship the true God together with their own gods and idols, but God is not pleased with this either. He wants **all** our love and worship. Some day He will put away all who worship images, Revelation 21.8, and He alone will be praised forever. In the old Hebrew Bible, the word *Amen* means *May it be so!* Here Paul agreed that God should be praised forever. You will see this word *Amen* in 9.5; 11.36; 15.33; 16.24,27, and many other places in the Bible.

26,27. Men love what is evil and so God gives them up to their own shameful passions. Instead of living a normal married life, many men and women become sexual perverts, and are called *homosexuals*. They soon receive in their own bodies the natural bad effects of these sins.

Notice that men and women **change** the glory of God, v.23, and worship images; they change the truth of God and believe a lie, v.25; and they even change natural relations between men and women for what is not natural, vs.26,27. As a result, God *gives them up* to evil desires, v.24; He gives them up to shameful passions, v.26; then He gives them up to corrupted minds, v.28.

These verses show the downward path which men have followed. Some people teach that men have always been seeking for the true God. They say that at first men did not know God, but they slowly began to worship spirits. Then they made images of these gods in the form of animals and men. After a long time some prophets of Israel got the idea that there was only one God, Jehovah. The Bible teaches that man is **not** seeking God, 3.11. At first men did know the true God, v.20, as in the days of Adam, Genesis 4.26. Some began to make images and worship them, v.23. They were worshipping creatures, v.25, really evil spirits, 1 Corinthians 10.20. Finally they did not want to think about God at all, v.28, and many today say there is no God.

But there is a God in heaven and He loves all men. Do

not try to argue with men who say there is no God; just keep telling them that God loves them.

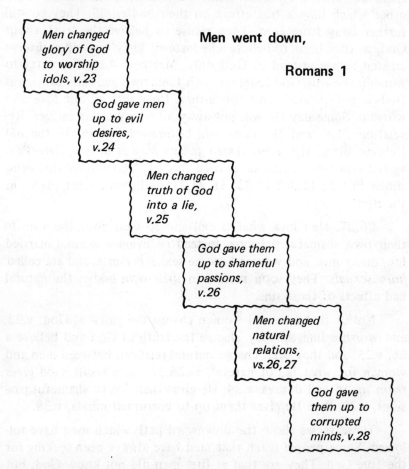

Men changed glory of God to worship idols, v.23

Men went down,

Romans 1

God gave men up to evil desires, v.24

Men changed truth of God into a lie, v.25

God gave them up to shameful passions, v.26

Men changed natural relations, vs.26,27

God gave them up to corrupted minds, v.28

1/9   We have seen the terrible things which men do, but here are more still. **28.** Men do not want God and He will not force Himself on them. He *gives them over* and lets them think what they wish, but He does not approve of their thoughts. They think they are free to do as they please, so they break all the rules. **29,30.** The Holy Spirit says they are full of evil, and nine evil things are listed here. They gossip and talk about other people in an unkind way. They hate God and do the things which He hates. (They also hate one another, Titus 3.3). They are not at all ashamed of their wicked practices, in fact, they are very proud of them, and think up new ways to do what is evil. God wants men to obey their parents, but they disobey. **31.** They do not understand God's ways, nor even try to. They do not keep their own promises and are not kind to others. **32.** They know that God is righteous and must judge these things, but still they keep on doing them. Worse still, they make friends of people who do the same.

These verses show what God says about men who forget about Him. Men today have made great progress in this world and done many wonderful things, but their hearts are no better; in fact, they are getting worse, 2 Timothy 3.13. Such people surely need the Good News that Christ died for their sins, and we should tell them. But perhaps you think that some men are better than these we have been reading about? Let us go on to Chapter 2.

1/10   **TEST YOURSELF ON CHAPTER 1**
   1. Which is the **shortest** of the seven parts of Romans?
   2. What is the main subject of the letter to Romans?
   3. Who are true saints today?
   4. Who would be Witness for Paul?
   5. Why was Paul proud of the Good News?
   6. What kind of men are righteous and have eternal life?
   7. How can people know God if they have never heard the Good News?
   8. What does God do to men who forget about Him?
   9. How do men live after they leave God and worship idols?
   10. Are there any verses in the Bible which prove that men are trying to find God?
   11. Some people do not obey their parents, or give thanks to God for their food. Are these things *sin*?
   12. Is Romans 1.18-32 *good news?*
   Check your answers on page 137

God will judge good men, 2.1-16

1/11   You would expect that the Righteous God will judge all sinners, but what about **good** men? Many people could read the list of terrible sins in 1.18-32 and think they had never done any of these things. They do not approve of people who commit such

24 *ALIVE AND FREE*

sins; in fact, they know what is sin and are quick to judge those who do these things. The first part of this section tells about the man who tries to judge others, and about God who will judge all men righteously.

Those who judge, 2.1-11

1. Some people think that they can pass judgment on others and so find an excuse for their own sins. Not so. They really judge themselves when they pass judgment on others, if they do the same things themselves. **2,3.** Everyone knows that God is the only righteous Judge of all men, and nobody can escape God's judgment just by acting like a judge himself. **4.** Such people seem to think that God's great mercy is unimportant. It is true that God does not judge every man as soon as he commits a sin, but many people suppose that He does not care what they do, so they go on and do more sinful things.

The Lord Jesus taught that we should not judge one another, Matthew 7.1. Judas tried to judge Mary when she poured some perfume on the Lord's feet, but the Lord told him to stop, John 12.7. The Holy Spirit also warned against judging others, James 4.11,12. However, the church must judge any Christian who commits sin, 1 Corinthians 5.

1/12   **5,6.** Many people keep on sinning and this hardens their hearts still more against God. They are only piling up more judgment for themselves. God will reveal everything on the Day of Judgment and will surely reward or punish every man for what he has done. **7.** Some try hard to please God; they want to go to heaven where no one will ever die. God will give them eternal life. **8.** Others like to argue and selfishly demand what they want. They refuse to believe what is true and to do what is right. They can expect only the terrible wrath of God. **9.** God's wrath will mean trouble and distress, and it will come on every person who does what is wrong, on Jews and all other people. The Jews heard the Good News first, 1.16, so they will be judged first if they do not believe. **10.** Others will receive glory, honour and peace, both Jews and Gentiles, if they believe and do what is right. **11.** Some men try to judge others, but God is always fair and will treat all men equally.

> *Glory, honour* and *peace,* v.10; these three words are found many times in Romans: glory, 16 times; honour, 6 times; peace, 11 times. Watch for these words as we come to them.

This part of Romans tells us how God will deal with men. He will judge all sinners and He will give eternal life to anyone who perfectly does His will, vs.7,10. We will soon see in chapter 3 that no one has ever been able to do this.

God will judge all men fairly, 2.12-16

1/13   **12.** God promised to give life to anyone who keeps His law perfectly, Romans 10.5; Galatians 3.12. He gave His law to the Jews, but many people had never heard of God's law, so they do not know this promise. They sin, they are lost and will die. The Jews have God's law and He will punish them for breaking it.

The word *law* is very important in Romans. We see it for the first time in 2.12, but it is found 19 times in this chapter, and 75 times in the letter to the Romans.

13. Many Jews thought that God would accept them just because He gave them His law. They could *hear* someone reading it every sabbath day, Acts 15.21, but this did not make them right with God. God wanted them to **obey** His law; if they had, He would have made them right with Himself. We will see that no one has ever done this, but God has a far better way to *justify* men, 3.20-24.

14. The Gentiles have not received the law which God gave to Moses, but they do many good things which the law requires. This shows that God has given all men some way of knowing what is right. This is in our *nature;* God gave us our *conscience.* **15.** If a man has the law of God it works in his mind to show that he is a guilty sinner, Romans 7.7; Galatians 3.19. Gentiles without the law have their consciences to help them know when they have done what is wrong. The conscience is a small voice in every man's mind. My conscience is *good* if I think that I have done nothing which is wrong, Acts 23.1; Romans 9.1; 1 Peter 3.16; if I have done something wrong, my conscience is *bad,* 1 Corinthians 8.7; Titus 1.15. A man may make himself believe that he has not done anything wrong, or he can make excuses for himself. For example,

Adam fell into terrible sin, but he tried to excuse himself by saying that it was Eve's fault, and that God had given her to him, Genesis 3.12. Saul tried to blame the people when he had sinned, 1 Samuel 15.17-21. **16.** No man will have any excuse on the day of judgment because God knows everything.

> The Good News is about the Lord Jesus Christ, 1.3; through the Good News, God can save anyone, 1.16; it shows that God is righteous and fair, 1.17. It also teaches that God has made the Lord Jesus Christ the Judge of all men, 2.16; John 5.22,23; Acts 17.31. We should warn men and tell them to come to Christ as their **Saviour** so that they will not have to stand before Him as their **Judge**.

God will judge the Jews, 2.17-29

Paul has been talking to every man who thinks that he has lived a good life, 2.1. Both Jews and Greeks should know that they are guilty in God's sight, 2.12. Now Paul began to speak to the Jew, any Jew, vs.17-24; then he explained what a Jew should really be like, vs.25-29.

The Jews are also guilty, 2.17-24

1/14   **17,18.** Paul was born a Jew and he was very proud of it before he knew Christ, Philippians 3.4-7. Here he spoke to every Jew who was proud of himself. The Jew

   (1)   depended on the law; he thought that he could rest on this fact, that God had given the law to Israel.

   (2)   He was proud and boasted that he knew the true God.

   (3)   He was sure that he knew what God wants men to do, even if others did not know.

   (4)   The Jew had learned what is good and right, in fact, he could choose the very best. Why?

   (5)   Because he had God's law.

19,20. The Jew did have God's law and this made him feel very proud. He was sure that he could

   (1)   guide others who were *blind* and did not know God.

   (2)   He could give light to men who were in the dark.

   (3)   He could teach other people because he was wise and they were foolish

(4) or like children.

(5) The proud Jew thought that he could understand the truth about God.

Paul used to be a Pharisee and he knew quite well how the Pharisees thought and felt, Acts 23.6. The Lord Jesus also knew what Pharisees were like. He once told a story about a Pharisee who was very proud of himself, Luke 18.11,12. This man prayed in the temple but his heart was not right with God. Here in Romans 2.17-20 Paul is speaking about the average Jew who trusted in the law of God but did not do all that the law required. He knows God's will, vs.17,18, and teaches others God's will, vs.19,20. Now the question is, Does he himself **do** the will of God? In fact, Paul asked **five** questions to show what the Jew should do:

21,22. This man should teach himself what is right before he tries to teach others. He would not do the sins which he tells others not to do. He knew from the law that men should not worship idols, Deuteronomy 5.7-10. Would he make a profit for himself from the temple of idols? The Greeks thought that "robbing temples" was a terrible sin, Acts 19.37, but the leaders of the Jews made huge profits from their own temple in Jerusalem. The Lord Jesus said they made the temple into a hiding place for thieves, Luke 19.46.

23,24. Yes, the Jews boasted because they had the law of God, but then they brought shame on God by not keeping the law, so the Gentiles said wicked things about the name of God. Long before this the prophets of Israel had told the people the same thing, Isaiah 52.5; Ezekiel 36.21-23.

What should the Jews really be like? 2.25-29

1/15 All Jews had to be circumcised. God told Abraham to cut off a little piece of the skin of every boy in his family eight days after he was born, Genesis 17.9-14. Circumcision was a sign that the little boy was under God's covenant. God told Moses that the people of Israel must always do this to every baby boy, Leviticus 12.3.

In New Testament times the Jews kept this command and the Lord Jesus was circumcised, Luke 2.21; John 7.22. [What must be done to a **Gentile** before he could belong to Israel? Exodus 12.48 _____] The Jews tried to force the Gentile Christians to be circumcised, Acts 15.5, but even in the Old Testament the Holy Spirit taught that it was really a matter of the heart, Deuteronomy 10.16; 30.6.

The word *circumcision* is found 14 times in chapters 2 to 4. The word *uncircumcision* is seen 11 times in these three chapters. In the rest of chapter 2 the Holy Spirit explains that a true Jew must keep the law.

25. Circumcision is a sign of God's covenant and it is a wonderful thing to be under the covenant of God. But many circumcised people break God's covenant by their sins and so their circumcision is of no value in itself. **26.** On the other hand, a Gentile may obey God's law and God will give him the blessings of His covenant. This man is not actually circumcised in his body, but his heart is right with God. **27.** He is better than the Jew who has God's law and is circumcised in a physical way, but breaks God's covenant by his sins. **28,29.** You see, God wants us to be **real** in our hearts. The one who really believes in God will have God's blessing whether he is circumcised or not. The word *Jew* comes from "Judah" whose name means *praise,* Genesis 29.35. The true Jew will obey God's law and the Lord will praise him and bless him.

The apostles baptized people who believed the Good News and became Christians, Acts 2.41. Some people today teach that you are not a true Christian until you have been baptized. This is wrong because anyone can become a Christian by believing in the Lord Jesus Christ. The Lord told the criminal that he would be in the place of great joy that very day, though he had never been baptized, Luke 23.43. Baptism is a sign to others that you have believed. God will accept a person who believes but has never been baptized and He will refuse many who have been baptized but are not true Christians in their hearts.

1/16 **TEST YOURSELF ON CHAPTER 2**
1. Why does God judge "good" men?
2. Some people think that they know God's law, and so they have a right to judge other men. Prove that God will judge them too.

3. God would give eternal life to those who really seek His glory, vs.7,10. Why then did Christ have to die?

4. How many times are these words found in Paul's letter to the Romans: Glory ......, Peace ......, Law .... What does this show?

5. The Gentiles do not have the Law of God; how can they know what is wrong?

6. Why did Saul blame the people of Israel for saving the sheep and cattle?

7. Why were many people proud that they were Jews?

8. What did Paul say to show that **having** the law was not enough?

9. What did the Lord Jesus say about the Jews who made a profit from the temple of God?

10. God told Abraham and Moses that all the men in Israel had to be circumcised. Does this law apply to Christians today?

11. Which is better in God's sight, a circumcised Jew who breaks God's law, or an uncircumcised Gentile who keeps the law?

12. In what way is circumcision like baptism?

Check your answers on page 137

God will judge all men, 3.1-20

1/17   We have seen that God will judge Gentiles because they know a little about God but do not try to please Him. He will judge the Jews because they have His law but do not keep it. Now we will see that the Old Testament Scriptures prove He must judge **all** men. But first the Holy Spirit answered four questions which someone might ask about this teaching, 3.1-8. We will see other questions in 4.1; 6.1; 7.1.

Questions and Answers

1. Paul has been proving that God will judge all men equally, so some might ask if the Jews have any real advantage over other men. If not, why should anyone be circumcised? 2. The Jew had many advantages but these came because he had the Old Testament. (We will read more about Israel's special blessings in 9.4,5.) God revealed Himself to the Jews for their own good and so they

would tell other nations about Him. The Jews kept the revelation safely, and we still have it today, but they failed to give it to all nations.

3,4. Many Jews did not believe God nor obey His law, but this cannot make God change His promises. They were not always faithful, but God is. He cannot change, Malachi 3.6; He cannot lie, Titus 1.2. Everybody in the world might agree on something but they would all be wrong if God said the opposite. One time David committed a terrible sin against God. At first he tried to tell himself that he had not done anything evil. But God kept speaking to him and David finally agreed that God must be right and he was wrong, Psalm 51.4. Daniel confessed his sins and the sins of Israel and said that Israel was in the wrong and God was righteous, Daniel 9.7. Here the Holy Spirit takes the words of David to show that God is always right.

> God has given us the Good News just as He committed the Old Testament to Israel. He has commanded us to take this message to all men. Today God's servants are preaching the Good News in many countries all over the world, but still millions of people have never yet heard about the love of God.

1/18   5. Men are not righteous and this shows more plainly that God is perfectly righteous. Someone might say that man's sin brings glory to God, and if so, why does God judge the sinner? This would make God appear to be unrighteous and Paul did not teach this at all. He only asked the question here because someone might want to argue in this way.

Think of a large piece of white paper with a yellow spot on it. You could not see the spot very well. Now put a black spot on the white paper and you can see it plainly, because the black and white are very different. This is a picture of man's wickedness and God's righteousness which are also completely different.

6. Of course God must judge the world righteously. 7. But someone continues to argue: I may tell a lie but this just shows that God is perfectly truthful. So my lie brings glory to God and why should He judge me for it? 8. Some would even say, "Let us do what is wrong because it will bring good." Indeed, some of Paul's enemies were saying that Paul preached in this way. But

Paul never taught anything like that and he knew that God would judge those who accused him falsely.

WHAT THE OLD TESTAMENT TEACHES

1/19   Now the Holy Spirit shows that the Old Testament proves all men are sinners. The Jews thought they had a better standing before God just because they had the Old Testament. **9.** The Jews had many advantages, v.2, but they were guilty of sin. Still they were no worse than others. All men, Jews and Gentiles, are under the power of sin, and we cannot deliver ourselves. The Holy Spirit in Romans 1 to 3 has proved that Jews and Gentiles are under the **judgment** of sin. **10-12.** The Jews trusted in the Old Testament, but these verses from the Old Testament show that **all** have sinned. God looks down on men; what does He see?

> No man is really righteous.
>
> No man understands God's ways or tries to find God.
>
> All have turned away from God, like servants who do not bring any profit to their masters, Matthew 25.30.
>
> No one always does what is good, not even one.
>
> [Which verses in Psalms 14 and 53 contain these words from Romans 3.10-12? ....]

All people are sinners, but some are worse than others. The Holy Spirit uses other verses from Isaiah and the book of Psalms to show how wicked some men are: their words, vs.13,14; their walk, vs.15,16; and their hearts, vs.17,18.

13,14. We use our throats, tongues, lips and mouths when we speak. Some men's throats are unclean like graves which are full of the bones of dead people, Psalm 5.9. Some men use their tongues to tell lies, and their lips to hurt others, Psalm 140.3. For example, men told lies about Naboth, 1 Kings 21.13, and he was put to death. Today some men seem to curse every time they speak, Psalm 10.7.

15,16. Their works are as bad as their words. They walk in an evil way; they kill some and make others unhappy, Isaiah 59.7,8. God commanded men to love others as they love themselves.

17,18. These wicked men seem to be happy, but they do not have real peace in their hearts. Secretly they worry about what will come next. They should fear God, but their works show that they just do not care, Psalm 36.1.

1/20   **19.** The next two verses are most important. They repeat in
short form what we have learned in this section of Romans, beginning at 1.18. We have seen that God is going to judge all men,
both Jews and Gentiles. The Jews rightly thought that they had
some special privileges. God had given them His law, but the law
proved that they were sinners, 2.23,24. Gentiles could not claim
before God that they were sinless, and neither could the Jews, 3.9.
No man that ever lived can stand before God and make excuses
or say that he has no sin. All men are under God's judgment.

<h2 style="text-align:center">ALL MEN ARE EITHER</h2>

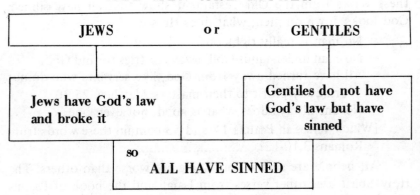

20. Many people have done some of the things which the law
requires, but not perfectly. Obeying the law does not put us right in
God's sight. We should obey God's commands **all** the time, not just
most of the time. A man becomes a sinner when he commits one
sin. Obeying the law for the rest of his life cannot change the fact
that he broke the law. For example, Cain murdered his brother
Abel, Genesis 4.8. We do not read in Genesis that Cain broke any
other law of God. Still he was a murderer. He could not bring Abel
back to life. The law of God makes men know that they are sinners;
it cannot make them right in God's sight.

Many people follow their own religion very carefully and
obey all the rules. The law of God cannot make anyone
right in His sight, and the laws of man's religion certainly
cannot do what God's law cannot. You ask, How then can
a man get right with God? Let us go on to the next verses.

GOD
CAN SAVE MEN
FROM THEIR SINS

3.21 - 5.21

1/21   Before we start this new section we should look again at the seven sections of Romans on page 9. In the second part, 1.18 to 3.20, we have seen that all men are guilty before God. Now the Holy Spirit will show us that God can forgive men, 3.21-5.21, **and** He can keep us from falling into sin again, chapters 6 to 8.

We have three parts in this third section:

1. God forgives men's sins if they believe, 3.21-4.25.
2. God gives many other blessings to those who believe, 5.1-11.
3. Christ is like Adam but far greater, 5.12-21.

God forgives men's sins if they believe, 3.21-4.25

The first part shows us how God can **justify** men, 3.21-31. For example, Abraham believed God's word and he was **justified**, chapter 4.

The word *justify* means to show that a person is just or right with God. It does not mean to make men righteous, because all are sinners. Nothing can change that fact. Also the Holy Spirit used the same word in speaking about God, Luke 7.29; Romans 3.4. Of course men cannot **make** God righteous, because He always has been righteous and always will be, but we can agree that He is righteous and show this to others.

A priest in Israel would examine a man who had some of the symptoms of a leper but did not really have this disease. The priest would declare that the man was clean so everyone would know, Leviticus 13.13. When God justifies us He declares we are just, then He gives us power to live a righteous life.

This word justify is used five times in 3.20-30 and altogether 15 times in chapters 2-8. We must think about this word very carefully and understand what the Holy Spirit means.

God justifies men, 3.21-31

In the rest of chapter 3 we see that God justifies men
by faith, vs.21,22
by grace, vs.23,24
by blood, vs.25,26

21. How can God be kind to men when He has declared that all men have sinned against Him? Do not think that God can put away His righteousness or act in a wrong way, even when He wants to be kind. God is the Great King and the highest Judge of the entire world. He must be fair, equal and righteous at all times. If He shows favours to one creature, He would have to do the same for all creatures. There is an enemy who loves to accuse God; he is called the Devil, which means the Accuser. If God ever did anything wrong, the Devil would be very happy indeed.

We have seen that all men are sinners and even God's law cannot make them right in His sight. Now we learn that God can be righteous and justify men without the law. The Old Testament does not clearly teach this great truth, but it really says the same thing. [What did the Lord Jesus call the Old Testament, Matthew 5.17; Luke 24.44?] We will see in chapter 4 that Abraham and David are examples of this teaching from the Old Testament.

22. God now reveals that His righteousness is for all men who believe. He can show that sinners are right with Him if they have faith in Christ.

23. The Jews thought that God's righteousness was only for them because they had the law. But we have seen that all men are sinners and so there is no difference. All men have failed to live as God required, they have fallen short of His *glory*. We can see the glory of God perfectly in the Lord Jesus Christ, John 1.14; 2 Corinthians 4.6. Who has lived up to this high standard? God cannot give men glory, He cannot honour them by saying that they have done what is right. Many men have not even tried to earn this honour nor come to Him to be saved, John 5.44; 12.43.

24. But now God can show that man is right with Him. Man cannot earn this by doing good or obeying any law - it is a free gift from God. The Lord Jesus made it possible because He died to set us free from sin, Ephesians 1.7; Colossians 1.14.

In old days wicked men often took people and made them slaves. A slave had to work all day without pay. He could not run away or do as he pleased. His master could sell him like an animal in the market. Sometimes a good man would buy a slave and then set him free.

The slave was a picture of the sinner because everyone who sins is a slave of sin, John 8.34,36. The Son of God came into this world to set us free. He paid the price for us by dying on the cross, 5.9.

1/22   **25.** There are three words here which we must look at very closely. (1) God **planned** long ago that the Lord Jesus Christ should die as an offering for man's sins, Ephesians 1.9. Now God shows or sets Christ before angels and men as the only means of saving people. (2) The Lord Jesus is the *propitiation* or *expiation* for our sins. This means that God the Judge is **satisfied** because the full price has been paid for our sins and for the sins of all men, 1 John 2.2; 4.10.

In Old Testament days the ark in the temple was a sign that God was with His people Israel. The ark was a box made of wood with gold on the outside and the inside. The gold cover on the top of the box was called the *mercy-seat* because it was the place of propitiation, Exodus 25.17; Hebrews 9.5. The high priest put the blood of an animal on the mercy seat once a year and God forgave the sins of the people, Leviticus 16.14,30,34. Two gold angels stood above the mercy seat and looked down on the blood. These angels speak of God's righteousness and the blood speaks of our Lord Jesus Christ who died for our sins. We see that God's love and righteousness meet together; this could only be in the cross of the

Lord Jesus. Christ is our *propitiation* or mercy-seat; God forgives
our sins through Christ.

(3) So God sets the Lord Jesus Christ before angels and men
to **prove** that He always was righteous even when He did not at
once punish men's sins in the past before Christ died. God was
patient and He had a plan. He knew that His Son would die for
men's sins. In the past God looked forward to the cross; now He
looks back to it.

IN THE PAST		NOW
God planned that	Christ should die to pay the full price for our sins.	*God proves to all* that He is righteous and always has been.

26. Now everybody can know that God is always righteous,
always was and always will be. In the past He seemed to let sins go
and did not always punish sinners at once. Now He can justify any
man who believes in the Lord Jesus, and show that he is right with
God. All this is possible because Christ died for all men.

We have learned that God is now able to justify men and show
that they are right with Him. (1) God planned this because He is a
God of grace; we are justified by *grace*, v.24. (2) Christ made it
possible because He died on the cross and paid the price. So we are
justified by His *blood*, v.25. This means it is possible for all men to
be justified, but it does not mean that all men are right before
God. What else is necessary? We are not told to keep God's law or
any other law to be justified, but it is necessary to believe God's
Good News, to accept Christ as your Saviour, and give yourself to
Him. We are justified by *faith*, vs.22,26.

It is not enough to believe in God or even to believe
about Christ. Have you ever received Jesus Christ into your
heart, accepted Him as your Lord and given yourself to
Him? If not, why not do it right now?

How can a man be *justified?*   Job 9.2

1. God's grace is for all men, vs. 23, 24	2. Christ died for all men, vs. 25, 26	3. Many men believe and so are *justified* by faith, vs. 21, 22	God gives them power to live a righteous life.
Justified by **grace**	*Justified* by **blood**	Many men refuse Christ; they are condemned.	They go on living in sin.

More questions and answers, 3.27-31

1/23   Paul knew that this teaching was new and many Jews could not believe what he was writing. He had often preached the Good News in Jewish meeting-places and had to answer questions which the Jews asked. Even so many Jews refused to believe this message, Acts 13.45; 28.23,24. Here we have three questions and the Holy Spirit's answers.

27,28. We have seen that men are justified by faith and not by works, vs.20,22. This truth does not give men anything to boast about. We could boast about our good works if God accepted them. But the Lord Jesus has done all the work, so we have nothing to boast about. We are justified by faith alone, not by keeping the law, or doing anything. The Holy Spirit repeats this very important truth in verse 28, which gives in short form the main teaching of 3.19-31.

29,30. But someone might say that God is the God of the Jews only, or that He is mostly interested in the Jews. Of course this is not true. There is only one God and He is willing to justify all men in the same way. He will justify any Jew on the basis of faith, not because he can keep the law. He will justify any Gentile also if he has faith in the Lord Jesus Christ.

31. Someone else might say, "You say that we are justified by faith and not by law. You are setting aside the law of God which He gave to His people." Is this true? Certainly not. The **law** says that the sinner has to die for his sins, Genesis 2.17; Ezekiel 18.4,20; Romans 6.23. The Good News says that Christ died for the sinner. So God upholds His own law, yet He can save anyone who believes in the Lord Jesus Christ. This is indeed **Good** News!

1/24   **TEST YOURSELF ON CHAPTER 3**

1. What was the main advantage of being a Jew?
2. Can any creature judge God, or be more righteous than God?
3, Is a man allowed to commit a sin, if it would bring a good result?
4, Some people live better lives than others. Will God accept really good people and take them into heaven?
5. What is the best excuse for a man when he must stand before God?
6. Suppose a man commits only one sin, and keeps the law all the rest of his life. Does he need this Saviour?
7. How can God justify a sinner?
8. This chapter says a man is justified by faith, grace, and blood. Which of these three came before the others in time?
9. We are slaves to sin; how does God set us free?
10. In what way is Christ like the mercy seat which covered the ark?
11. Are Jews better or worse than Gentiles?

Check your answers on page 138

The story of Abraham, chapter 4

1/25   The Jews thought that Paul was setting aside the law of God because he taught that a man is justified by faith. Paul showed that this was not true, 3.31, and now he gave the example of Abraham.

All Jews looked back to Abraham as a great man of God. [What does the Bible call Abraham? 2 Chronicles 20.7; Isaiah 41.8; James 2.23. The Bible does not use these words about any other man.] Here the Holy Spirit showed that Abraham himself was justified by faith, 4.1-8. Then He explained this truth still more in verses 9-25.

Abraham was justified by faith, 4.1-8

1,2. The people of Israel were the natural descendants of Abraham, Isaac and Jacob, whose other name was Israel. So the Jews asked Paul, "What about Abraham?" Paul agreed that Abraham could boast about his works **if** God justified him because his works were perfect. But Abraham could not talk about his works before God.

3. The important question is: What does the Bible say about it? For the believer this should answer all questions about God. We should thank God for revealing Himself in the Scriptures. The wisest man on earth cannot tell us any more about God than the Bible does.

Here the Holy Spirit used a verse from the Bible to prove that Abraham was justified by faith, Genesis 15.6. Abraham believed God: that was faith. God counted his faith to be righteousness: that was justification.

Notice the word **count**. Some Bibles say God *accepted* Abraham. Paul used this word 11 times in this chapter: vs.3, 4, 5, 6, 8, 9, 10, 11, 22, 23, 24. To be counted righteous means about the same as to be justified. Abraham was counted righteous because of his faith. This is the only way anyone can be justified.

4,5. If you go to work for anyone, he must pay you the wages which he promised. He owes you this money; it is not a gift. We cannot come to God and claim our wages. He created us and we owe everything to Him. We must come to God in faith and trust Him only and fully. God can justify any sinner who has faith. Of course God does not say that we are innocent, because we really are sinners. But He thinks about us in a different way and puts us on different ground: He says the price has been paid and we are free, 3.23,24. God sees that a man, a sinner, has faith. The sinner has no righteousness of his own, but God counts him as righteous if he has faith.

We have seen that the Old Testament really teaches that God can justify men by faith. The law and the prophets give their witness to this truth, 3.21. The **law** means the first five books of the Bible; the **prophets** wrote 21 other books. The other 13 books in the Old Testament include the book of Psalms and were called the Psalms or the *Writings,* Luke 24.44. The Holy Spirit has just given us the example of Abraham from the **law**, the first five books. Now He uses words of David from the Psalms.

1/26   **6-8.** These words prove that David knew this truth, that a man can be justified only apart from his works. He said that a man would be very happy

      (1) if God forgives the wrong things he had done;

      (2) if God covers his sins; and

      (3) if the Lord does not count his sins against him.

David knew what it means for a man to have sin in his heart which God has not forgiven. David committed several terrible sins and for a whole year he refused to confess to God. When he confessed, God forgave him and gave him joy in his heart again. David's story is in 2 Samuel chapters 11 and 12. David wrote Psalm 51 to show how he felt before God forgave him. He wrote Psalm 32 when he knew that God had forgiven him. Read carefully these two chapters in 2 Samuel and these two psalms.

In verses 6 to 8 we see three things: God *forgives* and *covers* sins and does not count them against the man who believes in Him. In Old Testament times God told His people to bring a sacrifice for sin, Leviticus 17.11. The blood of the sacrifice pointed forward to the death of the Lord Jesus Christ. Now God looks back to the cross of Christ. He can forgive sins **and** justify the sinner; justification is far greater and more wonderful than forgiveness. Why?

Adam was innocent in the Garden of Eden, but he could fall into sin and that is exactly what he did. God forgave Israel's sins, but they sinned again and then needed to ask God to forgive them again. When God justifies a man he is far better off than if he was only forgiven. A justified man might indeed fall into sin again, but he is still on the same ground before God. God did not put him on the ground of justification because of his own works and He will not take him off again because of his sins. This is indeed Good News! The Spirit says that a man is happy if the Lord will never

again count sin against him, v.6. God will never condemn the man
who is in Christ, 8.1.

　　　If a child of God falls into sin, the Father will have to
teach him and show him his sin. God does not put him back
into the place of a condemned sinner, but He does not let
him go on in sin either, Hebrews 12.5-11.

Paul explains these truths more fully, 4.9-25

1/27   *Every man must be justified by faith as Abraham was. We
have seen that no man is justified by works, vs.1-8. We now learn
that no man is justified because he is circumcised, vs.9-12; or because he keeps the law, vs.13-15. Abraham is called the father of
all who believe, vs.16-22. God told him he was justified and so we
can be sure that we are justified also, vs.23-25.*

9,10. David was circumcised when he was eight days old, as
all baby boys in Israel were. The Jews thought that God would
bless them just because they were circumcised, but we have seen
that this is not true, 2.25-29. Still someone might ask if God would
justify a person who did not belong to the nation of Israel. Could
such a person have the joy which David spoke of? Paul answered
this question by asking another: When did Abraham get this blessing? Was he justified before he was circumcised or after? Abraham
believed God and God counted his faith as righteousness, but he
was not circumcised until at least 14 years later.

Age	Abraham	Read this verse
75 years	He left Haran and moved to Canaan ...	Genesis 12.4
	He received God's promise and was justified	Genesis 15.5,6
85 years	He took Hagar as his wife	Genesis 16.3
99 years	He was circumcised	Genesis 17.1,26

*So there were at least 14 years between the time he
was justified and the time he was circumcised.*

His circumcision certainly was not the reason for his justification.

11. The circumcision was a sign to show that Abraham had a covenant with God, Genesis 17.11. It was also a **seal** to prove that God counted him as righteous. Kings put a seal on what they write so everyone will know that it is really from the king, Esther 8.8. Abraham is the first man who the Bible says was counted righteous and this was before he received the sign of righteousness. Therefore the Holy Spirit called Abraham the father of all who believe, even though they are not circumcised.

12. The Jews called Abraham their father, John 8.53, but here we see that all men, Jews and Gentiles, are the "children" of Abraham if they believe. The most important thing is that Abraham believed God and was justified. We can follow his example and walk in the same path of faith. If we do, we are justified before God and we are the "children" of Abraham.

Today many people think that they have to be baptized before God will justify them. These verses teach very plainly that faith and only faith is necessary. A person who believes should be baptized as a sign to others. The Holy Spirit is a seal or a sign to the man himself that he belongs to God, Ephesians 1.13; 4.30.

Will it help me if I keep the law? 4.13-15

1/28   Paul has shown that **works** will not help, vs.2,4,5,6. He has proven that **circumcision** is not necessary, vs.9-12. [How many times can you find the word *circumcision* in verses 9 to 12?] Now Paul turns to the **law.** (Note this word *law* five times in verses 13-16.

13. God promised Abraham that he would have the whole land of Canaan, Genesis 12.7; 15.18, and that all nations in the world would be blessed through him and his descendants, Genesis 12.3; Galatians 3.8. Abraham is the father of all Jews in a physical way and he is the father of all believers in a spiritual sense. Abraham's great descendant is the Lord Jesus Christ, Galatians 3.16. Christ will be King of the whole world, Psalm 2.8, and all believers will be with Him. Did God give this wonderful promise to Abraham because he kept the law or because he believed God? God gave His law to Moses about 400 years after this promise to Abraham, Galatians 3.17. It is true that Abraham obeyed God's commands and

God blessed him, Genesis 26.5, but He gave Abraham these promises because he **believed** Him.

14. Will God bless people because they keep the law? If so, faith is not important and God's promises would be of no value. God gave promises to Abraham and to us, not because we earned them but because He loves us.

15. Why then did God give His law when He had already given His promises? God's law does not bring His blessing but only His anger, because men cannot fully obey. His **promises** bring blessing because He Himself will fulfill His promises. The law brings God's anger on men because they break the law, but no one can break God's law before He tells him what to do. Men can sin and they do sin, but they do not break any law so they do not feel guilty. When they hear and know God's law they feel guilty and some ask God to forgive them. This is why God gave His law, so men would feel that they need a Saviour, Galatians 3.24.

Abraham is called the father of all who believe, 4.16-22

1/29   **16.** So God justifies a man if he has faith and believes. This is so that everyone will know it is all based on His grace. His promises are for all Abraham's descendants; to those who obey the law and to those who do not even know the law. Those who believe can be sure that God will fulfill His promises. Abraham believed God and so he is the father (in a spiritual way) of all who believe.

17. God gave this promise to Abraham when He changed his name. Abraham's name at first was *Abram,* which means "The great father", but God told him that his new name would be *Abraham,* which means "The father of many nations". God gave this promise, and Abraham believed Him; God stands by His word and fulfills His promise. God is able to bring dead people back to life and has done so a few times. When the Lord Jesus comes back, He will raise all men from death, John 5.27-29.

Do you think this is impossible? God created the world out of nothing, He formed man out of dust, Genesis 2.7, and He can certainly raise men from death. Abraham and Sarah were too old to have children when God promised that Abraham would be the father of many nations, Genesis 17.4; Hebrews 11.12. He had no descendants, not even one son, when God said his descendants would be like the dust and the stars, Genesis 13.16; 15.5. Later He promised that his descendants would be like the sand beside the sea, Genesis 22.17; Romans 9.27. God speaks about things which do not yet exist as if they existed already. He does this because He can give a command and it will take place at once. He said, "Let there be light" and there was light, Genesis 1.3.

18. Abraham and his wife Sarah were old and they could no longer hope to have any children. Still God had promised that they would have a son so they still hoped in God and believed His word. God had said that Abram would have very many descendants and so he became "Abraham", the father of many nations. **19.** Abraham was about 100 years old and Sarah was 90, Genesis 17.17. He knew that people as old as that could not have children. Still his faith was strong and he believed God. **20.** He did not ask any questions about God's promise and his faith became stronger still. This kind of faith brings glory to God. **21.** He was sure that God would not promise anything unless He was able to do it.

The word **God** means the Powerful One. Everything is possible for God, Matthew 19.26. A poor sick man knew that the Lord Jesus was **able** to make him better, but at first he was not sure if He would be willing to do so, Matthew 8.2. Abraham believed God was both able and willing to do what He had promised. Still even Abraham had a few doubts and once he asked God to put the blessing on his son Ishmael, Genesis 17.18. But this was not faith and so God told him once again what He had already promised.

In the New Testament God sent His angel to two people and promised them that they would have children. One was an old man, the other was a young woman who had no husband. Zechariah did not believe the promise and God punished him, Luke 1.18-20. Mary believed God and He blessed her, Luke 1.30-38.

God is glorified when we believe His Word and do what He commands. We can be very sure that He will keep all His promises. He has promised to save all who trust in the Lord Jesus; He has also promised to **keep** them. Let us be strong in faith and give God glory.

1/30   **22.** So the Holy Spirit repeated the words of verses 3 and 9, which come from Genesis 15.6. We have seen in verses 18 to 21 what it meant to Abraham to believe God's promise. God counted Abraham as righteous because of his faith.

Why did God tell Abraham he was justified? 4.23-25

23,24. These words in Genesis 15.6 must have made Abraham very happy, but they were written for us also. God will count **us** as righteous if we believe in Him, the God who has raised our Lord Jesus Christ from death. **25.** God gave His Son to die for our sins; God raised Him from death so He could show to all the world that He accepts us as righteous. God could not put us on the ground of righteousness unless the Lord Jesus paid the price. The Good News is this: Christ **has** died and God **can** accept as righteous all who believe. God the Son has done everything. Just believe and rejoice and thank Him.

2/1 **TEST YOURSELF ON CHAPTER 4**
   1. Could Abraham boast before God?
   2. What is the difference between gifts and wages?
   3. In Old Testament days, did believers know they were justified?
   4. In what way is justification better than forgiveness?
   5. Can a justified person do as he pleases?
   6. Why is it important to know when Abraham was circumcised?
   7. Who are the children of Abraham?
   8. How can God speak about things which do not exist as though they already existed?
   9. Was Abraham's faith perfect?
   10. Why did God raise Christ from death, v.25?

Check your answers on page 138

2/2   **God gives many other blessings to those who believe, 5.1-11**

   The third part of Romans shows us that God can save all men, 3.21-5.21. We have seen that God forgives men's sins if they believe, 3.21-4.25. God can justify us because Christ died for us. In chapter 5 we learn more about the blessings which we have through the death of Christ, vs.1-11. Then we will see that Christ is far greater than Adam, vs.12-21. [What is the full title of our Saviour in verses 1, 11, 21?]

In the first part of chapter 5 we see seven blessings which we receive because we are **justified**:

(1) We have *peace* with God, v.1. We were sinners like Adam and we were afraid of God, Genesis 3.10; we thought He was our enemy. Now we know that He loves us and has put us on the ground of righteousness. All the old fear is gone, we have peace in our hearts, peace with God. Some old Bibles say, *Let us continue to be at peace with God.* It is possible to start worrying or to doubt if God still loves me. Here the Holy Spirit tells us to keep on believing and to have peace with God. The Lord Jesus told us not to worry, John 14.1; it is a sin to doubt that God loves us.

(2) We receive another blessing through Christ: we can enter into the grace of God and stand there, v.2. This is a good place to stand. Once David prayed to the Lord and God put him on a solid rock, Psalm 40.2.

(3) We had no hope before we were saved, Ephesians 2.12, but now we have good reasons to hope. We can be sure that God will take us to be with Him in heaven. We will then see Christ in all His glory and we will share that glory with Him, 8.30.

This *hope* makes us happy now even when we have to go through times of great trouble, vs.3,4. A believer has peace with God, but he may have many troubles in this world. How can anyone be happy when he has a lot of trouble? We know that God loves us and wants us to be more like His Son. God will allow trouble to come into my life if it will make me more like Christ. The Lord Jesus endured many kinds of trouble but was always very patient, 1 Peter 2.23. The Holy Spirit will help me to be patient when I am in trouble. I should be happy to know that this experience will make me grow more like the Lord Jesus. God approves also and this makes my hope stronger still. I know that God will never fail or disappoint me in the end, v.5.

(4) God always loved men, but now He can show His *love* fully because Christ took away our sins. God loves in a special way those who love the Lord Jesus, John 14.23. The Holy Spirit makes

me know that God is pouring His love into my heart, v.5. The
Spirit also helps me to love others.

Christ poured out His blood for us   Matthew 26.28
The Holy Spirit was poured out on believers   Acts 10.45
The love of God is poured out in our hearts   Romans 5.5

2/3   **6-8.** God proves that He loves men because He gave His Son
for us. We men were entirely helpless and quite unable to save ourselves, 3.20. God waited hundreds of years and then sent His Son
just at the right time, Galatians 4.4. An ordinary person would not
give his life for another, even for a righteous man, but some might
be brave enough to die for a *good* man, v.7. A righteous man is
fair to other people and they will honour him, but a good man is
kind and people love him. God proved perfectly that He loves us
because Christ died for us while we were still sinners, neither righteous nor good.

> This also shows that we can come to Christ while we are
> still sinners. We do not have to wait until we make ourselves
> a little better. A good sinner is still a sinner. Good or bad,
> the Lord Jesus alone can save sinners.

(5) Another blessing from Christ: We can be sure that Christ
will *save* us from the wrath of God. Here and now we know that
God has justified us because of the blood of Christ which was
poured out for us, 3.25. The life of a man is in his blood, Leviticus
17.14. The Lord Jesus gave His life for us, His blood was poured
out and He died, John 19.30,34. In the future God will pour out
His great wrath on this world and on all those who do not believe
on His Son, John 3.36; Romans 1.18; Revelation 16.1. We will be
saved from God's judgment. [This is the first time we have seen the
word *saved* in Romans. Note also: 5.10; 8.24; 10.9,13.] It is a great
²/4 blessing to be sure you are saved. Verse 9 tells us that God has already justified us, and much more He will surely save us from
coming judgment.

(6) We were enemies of God, afraid of Him, and we disobeyed His laws. God always loved men, but now He has made us His friends through the death of His Son, v.10. We can be sure God loves us because He gave us His Son. This takes away all the old fear and we are *reconciled* to God. [Study this word *reconcile* in 2 Corinthians 5.18,19,20.] Much more, we can be saved every day by the Lord Jesus Christ. The Lord is alive today and is sitting on God's throne. He is praying for His people who are still in this world. He is able to save us from sin every day, Hebrews 7.25; 8.1. This is a great blessing, but the last is greater still:

(7) Our *joy* is in God Himself, v.11, not in our old sins, not in the things of the world, not in ourselves. Our greatest joy is not even in the gifts which God gives, but in the Giver, God Himself. God never changes, and so our joy in Him can last forever. This great joy comes through the Lord Jesus Christ, who has made us friends of God.

Christ died for wicked men	v.6
Christ died for us when we were still sinners	v.8
Christ died for us when we were enemies	v.10

Think again about these seven blessings which we receive from God because we are justified. Ask yourself if you are enjoying all these blessings. If not, believe that they are for you and thank the Lord for His love.

Abraham believed God, 4.3	and so do we, 5.1;
Abraham was made righteous with God, 4.3	and so are we, 5.1;
Abraham was a friend of God, James 2.23	and so are we, 5.10,11; John 15.15

Christ is like Adam, but far greater, 5.12-21

2/5   Many Jews did not accept Paul's teaching and wanted to go back to what Moses said. Paul went back further still and showed that Abraham was justified by faith, chapter 4. Now he went back still further, to Adam, and proved the Christ is greater than Adam.

Adam was the first man and the whole human race has descended from him. The Lord Jesus Christ is the Head of a new race which includes all believers. The Lord Jesus is called the last Adam because there will never be another race of men, 1 Corinthians 15.45.

12-14. The first Adam brought sin into the world and he died. All his descendants have the same nature; they commit sin and they die. Adam broke God's command, but God did not give the law to Adam's descendants until the time of Moses, about 2500 years later. People who lived during these years committed sin but they did not break the law. Still they all died because they had the same nature as Adam. Even today many little children die before they are old enough to know what sin is.

15. Adam was a picture or a figure or a *type* of the Lord Jesus Christ. Both are Heads of a Race. Both through one act had a great effect on many other people. But the acts of Adam and Christ are very different, and so is the effect on others. What were these two acts and their effects? Adam's terrible deed was committing the first sin; the effect of this sin is that all men die. The great deed of the Lord Jesus Christ was dying for our sins. The effect of this is that God can give eternal life to many people, all who believe. **16.** The sin of one man, Adam, resulted in the *condemnation* of the whole human race. But the grace of God and the death of Christ result in the *justification* or many sinners with their many sins. **17.** Again, it is certain that death ruled as a king over the entire human race, because one man sinned. It is now much more certain that many can receive God's grace and righteousness. Those who do will live forever and rule with Christ.

2/6   **18,19.** Here again the Holy Spirit repeats this great truth: One man, Adam, sinned; all men were condemned. One Man, Christ, died for sin; all men can be justified and receive life. One man, Adam, disobeyed God, many were made sinners. One Man, Christ, perfectly obeyed God; many will stand before God as righteous.

verse	One man, Adam		One man, Christ	
	Act	**Results**	**Act**	**Results**
15	Sin	Many died	Free gift	Many received grace
16	Sin	Condemnation	Free gift	Justification
17	Sin	Death ruled	Gift of righteousness	Many live and rule
18	Sin	All men condemned	One righteous act	Justification for all
19	One man disobeyed	Many made sinners	One obeyed	Many made righteous

20. God had judged all men as sinners, but people did not know it. God gave men His law so they would understand that they were sinners and some did learn what God really thought about them. But all men have received a sinful nature from their parents and so God's law just makes us want to sin all the more. So sin increased in the world but this was not God's will. God gave the law so men would know they were sinners. The law made men sin more than ever but it also taught many that they were sinners. God showed His grace to them. God's grace and Christ's death are more than enough for all the sins of all the men who ever lived.

21. Sin ruled like a king over men and all had to die. But now God's grace rules and we can have eternal life through our Lord Jesus Christ. And this is *through righteousness*. God does not set His law to one side so that He can save sinners. The price has been paid. His grace now rules over sin and death, and all this on a righteous basis.

Stop right now and give thanks to God for His wonderful plan of grace. Read these verses again and praise the Lord for all His love to you. Be sure you are not spoiling

God's plan. Some people refuse God's gift and try to *work* for eternal life. Just believe God's Word, accept Christ, and be happy.

2/7   **TEST YOURSELF ON CHAPTER 5**

1. What are the seven blessings in verses 1-11?
2. Which of these blessings is the greatest? Why?
3. How can anyone be really happy when he has trouble?
4. How can we be sure that God will save us from the coming judgment?
5. Why are we no longer afraid of God?
6. Why did Paul go back to Adam and teach about him in this chapter?
7. Why do innocent children die?
8. In what ways was Adam like Christ?
9. How was Adam different from Christ?
10. Why did God's law bring about more sin?

Check your answers on page 139

GOD CAN
KEEP US
FROM SINNING
chapters 6-8

We have seen some wonderful truth in the first three parts of Romans. All men, both Jews and Gentiles, have sinned and the law did not give the Jews a more favorable standing before God. God came in and provided a Saviour. The Lord Jesus died for God's enemies, but now we are friends because the old hate and fear are gone. We have a new standing before God: we are justified by faith. God will never judge us for our sins because His Son has already paid the price. God long ago justified Abraham, and he is the spiritual father of all who have faith in God. We are in Christ and have a new life; this is far better than being in Adam.

But what about the Christian who commits sin? The Bible gives four answers:

1. The man who is in Christ has a new life and does not **want** to sin.
2. Christ has risen from death and is alive today. He will give the Christian **power** to live the Christian life.
3. God has justified this man and will **not** judge him again as a sinner, but
4. God will chasten him or **teach** him if he continues in sin.

Now this part of Romans explains the second sentence: the Lord Jesus Christ can give us power to keep us from sin. He will deliver us from **sin**, chapter 6; from **law**, chapter 7; and from the **flesh**, 8.1-13. He will finally deliver us from this world and take us to **glory**, to heaven, 8.14-39.

Notice how many times these important words are found:

In	Chapter 6	Chapter 7	8.1-13
SIN is found	17 times	14 times	5 times
LAW is found	2 times	23 times	5 times
FLESH is found	once	4 times	13 times

Christ delivered us from sin, chapter 6

Sin is an important word in chapter 6. We should not sin because we are no longer dead in sin but **alive to God**, *vs.1-11; and because we are* **servants of God**, *not servants of sin, vs.12-25.*

Alive to God, 6.1-11

1,2. We have seen that God's grace is greater than all men's sins, 5.20. Some people would say this means that we may continue to commit sin because God's grace will also continue to increase. But this is not God's will at all; God never wants men to sin. Here the Holy Spirit tells us that we have died to sin and cannot live in sin any longer.

Dead to sin. Are these words true of Christians who are alive and are still often tempted to sin? No living Christian is perfect; we all are in danger of committing sin. But we are in union with Christ, who has died for sin. He has also died **to** sin, v.10. We can say that we have died with Christ, so we have died with reference to sin. This means that sin has no more claim over us.

> Before, we were dead in sin, because we were under the judgment of God. Now we are alive in Christ, but dead **to** sin. We have new life in us and should obey the Holy Spirit.

2/9 **3,4.** The Christians at Rome should have known what it means to be baptized. Every Christian enters into union with Christ when he first accepts the Lord. The Lord Jesus died, was buried, and rose again. The Christian is in union with Christ, dead, buried, risen. Baptism is a picture of this truth: the believer is put down into the water, stays there for a short time, and is brought up again out of the water. This shows people that he is in union with Christ. The believer himself should know that he has died in reference to sin and that God has raised him to a new life, just as He raised Christ from death. The Father had the power to raise Christ and He can use this same power to help me walk in a new way, and to live as a Christian should live, Ephesians 1.19,20. Christ was raised from death for God's glory; we should live and walk for God's glory in this world.

The Holy Spirit explained these things more fully in verses 5-11. **5.** We have been united with Christ when He died; we are united with Him in His resurrection. **6.** We should know that the old *self* was crucified with Christ on the cross. God wants to destroy the sinful habits in our bodies so we can become free to serve Him instead of sin. Before I was saved, I lived in sin and committed many sins every day. Every time a person commits a sin, it becomes easier to do it the next time, and it soon becomes a habit of his body and part of his nature. This person is under the judgment of death, but Christ died for him. We see that this old self was crucified with Christ so that these old habits of sin can be destroyed. We can be free from the power of the old sinful habits, and the old selfish nature, Colossians 2.11; 3.9.

2/10   **7.** The law cannot punish a person after he has died. A master cannot rule over his slave after he has died. As sinners we were under the judgment of the law; we were also slaves to sin. Now we are dead with Christ. This delivers us from the **penalty** of sin and the **power** of sin.

This verse does not mean that God will not punish sinners after they die. All men will rise from death, but only those who believed in Christ will have eternal life, John 5.28,29.

8. We also live with Christ. When the Lord comes we will be with Him forever, but even now we live because He lives, John 14.19. **9.** God raised the Lord Jesus from death and He can never die again. Death has no more power over Him. (Death never had any power over Christ, the perfect Man, until He took our sins on Himself. He was willing to give up His own life, John 10.18.) Now He is alive forever.

10. The Lord Jesus could only die once. He died with respect to sin, He settled the question of sin forever, Hebrews 9.26. Now He is alive forever, and He lives for God. **11.** We should think of ourselves in the same way. I am in union with Christ Jesus. He and I have died with respect to sin, it has no more claim over us. Christ lives for God's glory; so should I.

> Notice these three words: We **know**, vs.3,6,9; and **believe**, v.8, because these things are true. We should act according to these facts and **count** ourselves as dead and risen with Christ, v.11. We saw that God **counts** us as righteous, 4.3-5. We should think of ourselves as alive for God's glory alone.

Servants of God, 6.12-23

2/11   We were slaves of sin because we were born in sin and because we committed sin. Now we are free to serve God.

12. The Lord commands us not to let sin rule any longer in our bodies. These bodies are going to die, but we will get new bodies when the Lord comes, 1 Corinthians 15.53. We are allowing sin to rule us when we obey the natural desires of the body. **13.** We should never give any part of our bodies for the purpose of committing sin. We should not use our hands to take something which belongs to another person. We should not use our tongues to tell lies. Instead we should give our whole body to God because He has brought us out of death and given us the new life. We should also give all parts of the body to Him and use them only for doing what is right.

14. We can do these things because God has promised that sin will not rule over us. People who live by rules of law keep on falling into sin. We are now under the grace of God and are delivered from law and sin. In chapter 7 the Holy Spirit tells us more about law.

> [There are three commands in verses 12 and 13, but verse 14 is God's promise. Write out what we should not do and what we should do and note especially the promise of God.]

2/12   **15.** Again Paul asked the question which many unbelievers were asking. We live under the grace of God, not under law; does this mean that we can do as we please? Of course not. Read again

3.8 and 6.1, also Jude 4. **16.** We know that we are slaves of the
person we obey. Every time you obey makes it easier to obey again
and harder to disobey. We obeyed sin because sin was our master,
but this only leads to death. Now we obey God and do what is
right. Obeying God does not **put** us right with Him; only faith can
do that, 5.1. But when we obey God we are preparing for a great
day in the future. We will be glad then that we obeyed God now
while we live in this world. Our righteous acts will be like beautiful
clothes to wear in heaven, Revelation 19.8. **17.** Paul gave thanks to
God because the Christians were no longer slaves of sin. They
started to obey God when they gave themselves to God and accepted Christ as their Saviour. They were given over to this truth,
that they must not go on in sin. They obeyed this teaching gladly
with all their heart.

18. We were slaves of sin, but Christ set us free and we became
slaves of righteousness. Therefore we should do those things which

Sinner	DIED WITH CHRIST	Believer
condemned to die, 2.12		justified from the penalty of sin, 5.1
slave to sin, 6.16		free from the power of sin, 6.18

are right. **19.** Paul was speaking about slaves, and used words which
anyone could easily understand. Thousands of people were slaves
in those days. Their masters could kill them if they did not obey
or if they tried to run away. Of course no one wants to be called a
slave. But Paul knew how weak we are and how hard it is to break
the habits of sin. Still we **gave** ourselves to sin: our bodies and all
parts of the body. One sin led to another. First we practised little
unclean habits but still they were sins. We broke God's law once

and it became easier to keep on breaking it. Soon we were *slaves* to sin. Now we must give ourselves to God, and all parts of our bodies as well. We will do what is right and in this way we will learn to be holy. First I should judge everything I do. If it is wrong, I should confess it to the Lord Jesus. This is the **righteous** life. Soon I will know what is wrong *before* I do it. I learn to turn away from sin and not give in to it. This is the **holy** life.

> For example, Judah fell into terrible sin. He confessed that he had done a very wrong thing and we never read that he fell into that sin again, Genesis 38.26. If he had not judged himself he would have done the same thing again. We should judge our own sins and turn from them.

2/13   **20.** We were slaves of sin and did not obey the commands of a righteous God. **21.** What good did sin do for us? What value did we get from the life of sin? We thought we were happy but now we are ashamed of the things which we used to do. Now we know that sin leads to death and we are sorry that we sinned so much against God. **22.** Now we are free from the power of sin. We are still slaves but now slaves to God, not to sin. This means we can live a holy life instead of practising unclean habits. Right now we have eternal life, John 3.36.

23. Men who serve sin must receive sin's wages, which is death. God gives eternal life to all who are in Christ Jesus, all who receive Christ as Saviour and Lord. This life will never end, just as God has no end, 16.26. It is the life needed for heaven. Read again 2.7; 5.21; also Galatians 6.8; 1 Timothy 1.16; 1 John 5.11,13.

> It is important to know that eternal life is a **gift** from God, 5.15,16; 6.23. Many people think they have to do good works to earn eternal life, but no one can buy his way into God's home in heaven. The younger son wanted to go back to his father as a hired worker, but the father received him as his son, Luke 15.19,22-24. It cost God everything to provide eternal life: He gave His only Son. The Lord Jesus became poor so we can be saved, 2 Corinthians 8.9. God offers us eternal life as a **gift**. Do not dishonour God by offering to pay a little for what He wants to **give** you. Just believe Him and accept eternal life as His gift to you.

2/14 **TEST YOURSELF ON CHAPTER 6**

1. The Bible teaches four things about a true Christian who falls into sin. Which of these is explained in Romans 3.21 - 5.21?
2. *Sin, law, flesh.* Which of these three words is found most often in Romans 6? .... ; in Romans 7? .... ; in Romans 8? ....
3. We *were* dead .... sin; we *are* dead .... sin.
4. How am I buried with Christ?
5. Does verse 7 mean that dead people are free from the penalty of their sins?
6. When did death have any power over the Lord Jesus Christ?
7. God counts us as righteous; how should we think about ourselves?
8. Which part of our bodies may we keep for ourselves?
9. Is the Christian still a slave?
10. Can men refuse their wages after they have served sin?
11. Why did the father in Luke 15 receive his younger son as his **son**, and not as a hired worker?

Check your answers on page 139

The Lord delivers us from the law, chapter 7

2/15   Most of the people who lived in Rome were Gentiles, but many Jews lived there too. The church at Rome was probably started by Jews who had gone to Jerusalem and believed in Christ on the day of Pentecost. The Holy Spirit often used the Old Testament to prove some of the truths which He taught in this letter to the Romans (see page 14).

We have seen that the Gentiles are guilty of great sin, 1.18-32, and that the Jews break the law, 2.17-29. Many Jews and Gentiles believed the Good News and God forgave them, 10.12. We have also learned that God can deliver Gentile believers from sin (and **all** who believe), chapter 5. Now we will see that God can deliver Jewish believers from the **law**, chapter 7.

The word *law* is found 23 times in this chapter. Any law has a claim on men as long as they live, but not after that, vs.1-6. The law of God is important to show men that they are sinners, vs.7-13. The law cannot make us perfect because we are too weak to obey all that it says, vs.14-20. God can also deliver us from our own weakness, vs.21-25.

How long can law make a claim over men? 7.1-6

1. The people of Rome had very good laws and even today many countries follow the old Roman laws. The Jews in the church of Rome also knew about the Old Testament law which God gave to Moses. No law can make a claim on a man after he has died.

Paul called the believers *brothers*. He used this word 11 times in Romans and in many other letters of the New Testament. [Which of these verses does **not** have a word meaning *brothers?* 1.13; 7.1, 4; 8.12; 9.1; 10.1; 11.25; 12.1; 15.14,15,30; 16.17.]

It is wonderful to belong to the family of God. God is the Father of all who have been born again and have the new life in Christ. We are all brothers and should help each other to serve the Lord.

2,3. In verse 1 Paul stated a general rule and in verses 2 and 3 he gave an example. The law says that a married woman is bound to her husband as long as he lives. Some women live with other men before their husbands have died: they are guilty of adultery, like the woman in John 4.18. When the husband has died, the wife can marry someone else. For example, David married Abigail after her husband Nabal had died. She was not guilty of adultery, 1 Samuel 25.39.

2/16 **4.** We were bound to obey the law until death. The law is not dead but we have died, with Christ. The *body* of Christ here means His death, Hebrews 2.14; 10.10. Now we are free from the law and all its claims. We are joined to Christ and can bear fruit for God's glory. A married woman can have children; the believer is joined to Christ and can bring other people to Christ. If they believe they

become children of God. This is what it means to bear fruit,
1.13; 6.22.

God wants us to bear fruit for Him, John 15.8. The fruit
of the Spirit is love, joy, peace and other wonderful things,
Galatians 5.22,23. It is not possible to have these things if
we live in fear all the time. Many Christians are afraid of
breaking God's law. Here the Holy Spirit shows us that
we are now free from the law so we can bear *fruit* for
God's glory.

5. Before we were saved we lived according to our old nature,
the flesh, 8.8,9. This old nature will not obey God. God says we
must not do something and the old nature at once wants to do it.
You see that the law stirs up our own natural desires in our bodies
and makes us want to sin. The result is death because committing
sin leads to death. **6.** Now we have died with Christ and therefore
we have died to the law. Because of death (Christ's death) we are
free from the law, like the woman in verse 2. The law cannot rule
over us any longer. We are free to serve God, not by keeping rules
or laws, but in the power of the Holy Spirit.

We cannot be justified or saved by keeping the law, 3.28.
And we cannot live a good Christian life by keeping rules of
law. Only Christ can save us and only the Holy Spirit can
make us live our lives as God wants us to.

Why did God give the law? 7.7-11

2/17   *The law stirs up my old nature and makes me want to sin, but*
this does not mean that the law is evil in itself, v.7. The effect of
the law is to make men know what sin is, v.7; to make sin "live",
v.8; and to make sinners "die", vs.9-11.

7. The law makes me want to sin, but the law itself is not sinful. However the law tells me what is sin because it shows me what
God wants me to do. For example, the law says that I should not
covet anything which belongs to someone else, Exodus 20.17.
When I hear this, I know that it is sin to want very hard what
other people have. Paul told us what happened to him, but these
things are true of all of us, we are all the same.

8. Sin lives in every man, but for years we did not know it.
Then God gave a command and we at once wanted what we should

not have. Sin in me uses the command to make me covet or very much want all kinds of evil things. Sin does not act in me until I know the command. Paul is speaking here of himself and of any man before he is saved.

The word *commandment* is used seven times in Romans: six times in this chapter and once more only in the rest of the book, 13.9. The word *law* includes many small but important commandments, Matthew 5.19.

9. I was "alive", I thought I was happy, because I did not know that I was separated from God. When I heard God's command I learned that *sin* in me was very much alive. I also learned that I was really dead because I was far from God. A man is naturally dead if his body is separated from his soul or spirit, James 2.26. The Bible says that he is spiritually dead if his spirit is separated from God, Ephesians 2.1. **10.** God gave commands and laws so that men might obey and live, Leviticus 18.5. But law brings out the sin in me, and sin leads to death. **11.** Again Paul said that sin uses the command to lead me into sin, v.8. Satan deceived Eve in the Garden of Eden, Genesis 3.13; 1 Timothy 2.14. She broke God's command, she led Adam to sin, and they both died. Since then every person has been born with a sinful nature. God says DON'T and I want to do it. So the law means that I must die for my sins.

The law is good, 7.12,13

2/18   **12.** God gave the law and the commandments to Moses. God is holy, God is righteous and He is good. The law itself is like God who is the Law-Giver. The law is *holy,* it shows us what is sin. The commandment of God is *righteous,* it teaches that God must judge sin. It is *good;* it teaches us these things so we will turn to God. **13.** But Paul has just said that the law brings death, v.10; is that good? The law is good and God gave the law so that men would know how terrible sin is. People do not understand how bad sin is. But sin works through the good commandment and I learn that I must die. Now I can see that sin cannot make me happy. The good commandment teaches me that sin is very bad.

Why is the law weak? 7.14-20

The law makes me understand that I am a sinner and that sin is very bad in God's sight. It shows me that I must die for my sins.

The law is good, but it cannot make me good. Why is this? It is because I am sold like a slave to sin, vs.14,15; sin lives in me, vs.16-20.

2/19   14. God is Spirit and He gave man a **spiritual** law. We men have both body and spirit but most of the time the old nature rules us and we do not follow the spirit. We are slaves to sin, like people who are sold as slaves.

>   The king of Israel sold himself to do evil, 1 Kings 21.20; and so did the people of Israel, 2 Kings 17.17. Sin seems to be pleasant for a short time, but it leads to eternal judgment, Hebrews 11.25; 6.2.

15. Paul was speaking of the struggle in his own heart. He knew he should always do what is right, but he kept doing what he hated to do.

16. Paul agreed that the law was good, but he did the things which he knew were wrong. 17. This shows that Paul's new nature did not keep doing what was wrong, but it was the sin that also lived in him. Still Paul was responsible for what he did, and so are we.

God gave	the LAW	to Men
	The LAW is *good*, v.12	
	but it brings	*death* to men, v.10
		because men are weak, v.16

18. The old nature in every man is called the *flesh*. No good thing is in the flesh: it is all evil. The Holy Spirit lives in us, in our bodies, but the word *flesh* here means our old nature. We cannot do good, even if we want to, unless the Holy Spirit helps us.

Some people try to make themselves good, or better. Some think they will be able to do good if they try very hard, or go to school, or give up something. But God says there is no good thing in the flesh. If you believe God you will not try to make the flesh any better.

19. Paul admitted that he did the evil things which he himself did not want to do, but he did not practise the good things which he really wanted. **20.** This proves that he was not acting from himself, but was moved by another force inside him. This was sin which lived in Paul and lives in every one of us.

God can deliver us from our own weakness, 7.21-25

Our God can save us and forgive our sins. He can also keep us from sin, chapter 6, and deliver us from the law, 7.1-20. He can help us although we are weak, 7.21-25, and save us from the flesh, 8.1-13. He is *able to keep* us, Jude 24.

First we see that there are two laws, vs.21-23. The word *law* sometimes means what we **should** do; if we don't we will be punished. For example, the government says you must pay your taxes; if you don't you will go to prison. The law of God says you must obey Him or He will punish you.

The word *law* is also used for something which always happens. For example, if I drop something it always falls to the ground. This is called the *law of gravity.*

2/20   In Romans 7 we have seen that God's commandment makes me want to sin. In verse **21**, this is called a law or principle. **22.** Paul also had a new nature, and this new nature in him was happy to obey all of God's law or commands. This new nature makes us like Christ: the Lord Jesus was always most happy to do His Father's will, Psalm 40.8; Hebrews 10.9.

23. But Paul said again that the old law of sin was still in him. It was different from the law of his mind, because his mind approved God's law. So there is a struggle in everyone of us. Sometimes it seems that the old sinful nature always wins.

24. No wonder Paul was unhappy! He asked who would deliver him from the power of sin which lived in his body. He could not win the victory even when he tried very hard. **25.** It is not God's will that His children should be unhappy and it is certainly not His will that we should go on sinning and failing. God and only God can and will deliver us from the power of sin through our Lord Jesus Christ. Paul gave thanks to God and so should we.

The letter to the Romans tells us God's Good News, 1.15,16, but the good news of chapter 7 is found in the first part of the last verse. The last part of this verse tells us again in short form what we have learned in chapter 7. We can serve God with our new nature, but our old nature can serve only sin.

Paul spoke of himself as a man in chapter 7, but we all have the same experience. In verses 7-13 Paul tells us what happened in past time, before he was saved. In verses 14-25, he speaks of his experience as a Christian with two natures. Notice what Paul **did**, v.15: he sinned because of what he **was**, v.18. Soon he **found** a law or principle, vs.21,23, and so he felt he **needed** a Saviour, v.24.

Christians who know this chapter do not need to go through the same experiences that Paul did. We should know that we have two natures; that the flesh is evil and we cannot win the victory over it; but God will deliver us through the Lord Jesus Christ.

2/21   **TEST YOURSELF ON CHAPTER 7**

1. How long does the law have claim on anyone? Give an example of this.
2. Is a Christian bound to keep the law? Why?
3. We can say we are married to Christ. What is the *fruit* of this marriage?
4. How can a Christian serve God?
5. How does God's command result in death?
6. What is spiritual death?
7. If God's law results in death, why did God give it?
8. Many people think that God will accept them if they only obey the law. What is wrong with this theory?
9. The words *I* and *me* are found 24 times in verses 14-20. Is Paul talking about himself?
10. Does God try to make our *flesh* better?

Check your answers on page 140

The work of the Holy Spirit, chapter 8

2/22   The Holy Spirit is referred to 20 times in chapter 8 and only eight times in all the other chapters of Romans. Who is the Holy Spirit? There is only one God, the eternal Creator of all else, but the Bible speaks of God the Father, God the Son, and God the Holy Spirit. The Holy Spirit is not just a power or force; He is a Person, He is God. He has given us the Bible, 2 Peter 1.21. Every believer has been born again and has received new life from the Spirit, John 3.5. In Romans 8, He delivers us from the power of the flesh, our old nature, vs.1-13. He also makes us sure that we belong to God, vs.14-39.

Deliverance from the flesh, 8.1-13

When God saves us, He delivers us from the power of sin, chapter 6, and from the power of the law, chapter 7. He also saves us from the power of the flesh, 8.1-13. We can obey God's law through the power of the Holy Spirit, vs.1-4. We should think about what the Spirit wants us to do, vs.5-8, because we have life through the Spirit, vs.9-13.

We can obey God's law, 8.1-4

1. Let us go back to chapters 1, 2, and 3 and remember that God has already judged all men and declared that the whole world is guilty before Him, 3.19. God has condemned all men because all have sinned, 5.16,18. But the Lord Jesus has paid the penalty for our sin, 3.24-26, and now the Holy Spirit tells us there is *no condemnation* for all who are in Christ Jesus.

No condemnation is the same as *justification,* which is far greater and better than the forgiveness of sins, see pages 34 and 40. But it is only for those who are in Christ Jesus. How do you get into Christ Jesus? The Spirit does not say that justification is for those who have been baptized or who join the church or pay money. When you receive Christ into your heart, John 1.12, He receives you, John 6.37. God at once puts you on the ground of justification and there is therefore now *no condemnation* for you.

(Some old Bibles add a few words to verse 1, which teach that something else is necessary before God will justify those who are in Christ Jesus. These words are properly found at the end of verse 4. Every person who is *in Christ* should walk according to the

Spirit but God will not condemn him again as a sinner, even if he walks according to the flesh.)

2. The Holy Spirit gives us the new life and here He is called the *Spirit of life.* The law of sin and death is the rule or principle that sin in me gains the victory and sin leads to death, 7.13,21,23. The law of the Spirit is the principle or rule that the Holy Spirit gives life to those who are in Christ Jesus. The law of the Spirit is not a new set of commands which I must obey to be saved.

3. We have seen that the law cannot make men do what is right because all men have the old nature, the *flesh,* 7.14. God can now do what the law cannot do. He sent His only Son into the world to become a Man. God never created the Son; the Son of God is eternal like the Father. The Son was born as a Man, John 1.1,14. He looked like other men but He did not have a sinful nature and He never sinned. The perfect life of the Lord Jesus Christ shows what God wants, and how far short we have fallen. We have all sinned in our bodies of flesh and we feel guilty and condemned when we consider Christ's life. God sent His Son to be an offering **for** sin. When the Lord Jesus died on the cross, God showed to all that He hates sin and He must judge sin. So God condemned sin by both the life and death of our Lord Jesus Christ.

4. The law required that the sinner must die, but Christ died instead. For believers the law has been fulfilled. The Lord Jesus fulfilled the law while He lived by obeying every command. When He died the righteous demand of the law was fulfilled. Now we believers fulfill the law **if** we walk and live in the Spirit and not according to the flesh. The Holy Spirit wants us to obey God and the Holy Spirit leads us to obey God. He makes us want to obey and He gives us the power to do so.

So God's law is honoured. It could not make the natural man obey, but the real Christian obeys God's law, unless he walks and lives according to the flesh.

We should think about what the Spirit wants us to do,8.5-8

2/23   The Holy Spirit is able to tell us what to do. We should think about these things, not the desires of the flesh.

5. Before we were saved we lived according to the flesh, according to our old human nature. The flesh controlled our minds and we kept thinking about the things which the flesh wanted. Now we still have the flesh in us but we also have the Spirit of God. We should live and walk according to what the Spirit wants. If we do, He will control our minds and we will think about things the way He wants us to think. This means we will love God and men, we will hate sin and evil. We will think about things which are pure and good, Philippians 4.8.

6. Some people keep thinking about what the old flesh wants. This is sin, and sin results in death; these people are far from God. We should think about things which the Holy Spirit wants us to do. Then we will know real life and true peace in our hearts. 7. Those who keep thinking about the flesh show that they are really enemies of God in their hearts. These people do not obey God and they do not want to. In fact they are not **able** to obey and they cannot change their own hearts. 8. They who are *in the flesh* are slaves to their own nature and so they cannot do those things which please God. *Without faith nobody can please God,* Hebrews 11.6.

> Esau was a man who lived for himself and followed the desires of the flesh. He did not want God's blessings, Hebrews 12.16,17; he hated his brother Jacob, and took four Gentile women for his wives. These things did not please God.

We have life through the Spirit, 8.9-13

2/24 *All true believers have the Holy Spirit. He gives us both life, vs.9-11; and victory over sin, vs.12,13.*

9. Paul was sure that the Christians at Rome lived according to the Spirit, v.5; they allowed the Holy Spirit to control their minds, v.6; and were really *in the Spirit,* v.9. These things can be true of all people if the Holy Spirit lives in them; and the Spirit lives in all who belong to Christ. There is only one Holy Spirit; in this verse He is called the Spirit of God and the Spirit of Christ. [Read John 14.16,26; 15.26; 16.7, and consider Who is said to *send* the Holy Spirit.]

> Some Christians do not know the truth of this verse and are afraid that they do not have the Holy Spirit. But here we learn plainly that those who do not have the Spirit do not belong to Christ, they are not saved at all.

10. Christ is in every believer and the Holy Spirit is in everyone who believes, John 14.17,20. Our bodies are going to die because of sin, but we have been born again. The Holy Spirit has given us spiritual life because God has justified us, v.1, and we will never be judged as sinners. **11.** God raised the Lord Jesus from death, 4.24,25; 6.4,9; 7.4, and God's Spirit lives in us. Therefore God will raise us from death when the Lord comes back again, 1 Thessalonians 4.16,17. Those who are still alive will be given new bodies which can never die. We can be sure of these things because the Holy Spirit lives in us, 2 Corinthians 1.22.

12. Because these things are all true, we are free from all the claims of the flesh. The flesh has no good thing in it, 7.18; it leads me into sin and sin brings death. **13.** Many people think that real life means they can do as they please. They live according to the desires of their natural bodies and this leads to death, eternal separation from God. We have the Holy Spirit and by His power we can put these old habits to death. Real life is victory over sin.

We can know that God will take us into the glory, 8.14-39

God has justified us and the Holy Spirit has given us power to live for Christ in this world. We next learn that we have a wonderful future and we are sure that God will give us great glory with Himself. We are sons of God, vs.14-17, and all the world will know it when Christ comes back again, vs.18-25. Even now God our Father will answer our prayer, and He will make us more like Christ, vs.26-30. Nothing can ever separate us from God's love, vs.31-39.

We are the sons of God, 8.14-17

2/25   The Spirit of God shows us each one that we are God's children, and we will share Christ's possessions with Him.

14. The Holy Spirit works in people of the world when He proves to them that they are sinners, John 16.8. He tries to lead them to God. If they follow the Spirit, they will believe on Christ and become children of God. We believers will fulfil the law if we walk in the Spirit, 8.4. We could not do this before we were born again, so the Holy Spirit in us makes us certain that we are God's sons. Other people can see that the Holy Spirit is leading us and they too will know that we are in God's family. For example, we should love our enemies and do good to them. This shows that we are like the Father, Matthew 5.44,45.

[What will happen to God's children when Christ comes? 1 John 3.1,2.]

15. A slave may be very much afraid of his master and most people are afraid to die, Hebrews 2.15. We have received the Holy Spirit and are no longer afraid of God. The Spirit in us leads us to call God *Father,* like a little child who trusts his own father perfectly without fear, Galatians 4.6.

The Holy Spirit has made us to be sons of God, but in this verse Paul spoke of the future time when God will show to all His creatures that we are His sons, v.23. Today we ought to walk and act so that people will know that we are God's children.

16. Now the Holy Spirit and my own human spirit both witness that I am a child of God. Some old Bibles say *the Spirit itself* but the Holy Spirit is a Person and we should say the Spirit *Himself.* Every man has his own spirit as well as his body and soul, 1 Thessalonians 5.23. I know that I am a child of God and the Holy Spirit makes me sure about this.

17. Since we are children of God we are *heirs* of God and will share in the rich blessings which God has prepared for us, 1 Corinthians 2.9. The Father has given all things to His Son, Matthew 11.27, and the Son shares everything with God's children, 1 Corinthians 3.21. But now every Christian suffers because he belongs to Christ. Some try to avoid it, but those who gladly share Christ's sufferings will share more of His glory.

In most families the sons do not get a share of the father's property until he has died. God's children get their great blessing from One who can never die; and through the Lord Jesus Christ, who has already died and risen again.

The Lord Jesus suffered in two ways:

(1) from men who hated Him because He was the Son of God; and

(2) from God, when He paid the price of our sins.

We can never share in the sufferings of Christ for sin, because He did all the work Himself. We can and should suffer with Him while He is rejected by the world.

[To whom was the Lord speaking in John 7.7? .... In John 15.18-20? ....]

The world will know that we are the sons of God, 8.18-25

2|26   *The Holy Spirit makes me sure, that I am God's child, and other Christians can know that I belong to God if they see that I follow the Spirit's leading. When the Lord comes, all the world will see Him, Revelation 1.7, and they will see us with Him. The day of glory is coming, v.18, and everything that has been created is waiting for that day, vs.19-22; we believers are waiting for that day too, vs.23-25.*

18. Paul had suffered a great deal for the Lord Jesus Christ, but he knew that the coming glory will make all the suffering seem like nothing. This was not just Paul's opinion, because the Holy Spirit led him to write these things. We will not have to suffer as much as Paul, but when we suffer for Christ we should remember that we will soon share in His glory.

19. God created all animals and the whole world. Animals do not have a spirit and they cannot know God as men can. But the whole creation will be greatly blessed when the Lord comes to rule over the earth. At that time God will show to all that we are the sons of God.

20. When Adam fell into sin, the whole creation was affected. God cursed the ground because of Adam's sin, Genesis 3.17. Before Adam sinned he gave names to all animals, Genesis 2.19, but after that, many animals became wild. In the garden of Eden, God planted beautiful fruit trees, but after Adam fell into sin, thorns grew up, Genesis 2.9; 3.18. Here in Romans we see that the world of nature is not now as beautiful or as wonderful as it is going to be.

21. The whole world of nature is always changing and decaying. Flowers, trees and animals spoil and die. When the Lord comes, wild animals will no longer kill other animals, but will eat grass like cattle. There will be plenty of water in the desert and flowers and food will grow there, Isaiah 11.6; 35.1,2,7; 65.25. The whole creation will be blessed when man is blessed. Creation will be set free from its present condition when we enter our new freedom. **22.** From the time that Adam sinned until now, the whole world of nature has been in pain and sorrow, like a woman just before her baby is born. This sorrow will suddenly end when the Lord comes.

2/27   **23.** Men and women have also had to live in sorrow and work hard ever since Adam and Eve-sinned, Genesis 3.16-19, and this is is equally true of believers. However, we have the Holy Spirit, who is like the first part of a great harvest of blessing. God has already given us the Spirit and we know that God has much more to give us later on. God has made us His sons but we are still groaning in sorrow. We are sure that God will soon show the whole world that we are His sons. Already we have been redeemed and set free from the penalty of sin. Soon our bodies also will be changed and made like Christ's body, Philippians 3.21.

24. We have been saved by faith in the Lord Jesus Christ, Acts 16.31, but we are not yet in heaven. We *hope* that God will some day take us to heaven. The word *hope* in the New Testament means what we expect will take place in the future. We are very sure that the Lord will take us to heaven because He has said so in the Bible. When the Lord comes we will not *hope* to see Him because we will actually see Him at last. **25.** For the present time we should wait with patience for the Lord to come, even when we have a good deal of trouble.

There are three things which we need while we are in this world: faith, hope, love, 1 Corinthians 13.13. Love is the greatest because it will last forever.

God will answer our prayers and make us more like His Son, 8.26-30

2/28 *The Holy Spirit helps us to pray, vs.26,27, and God is working for our good, vs.28-30.*

26. We all need patience, Hebrews 10.36, and the Holy Spirit can give it to us. We are weak in many ways but He will always help us. The Lord has promised to answer our prayer, but sometimes we do not know what to pray for. It is quite possible to ask for the wrong thing, James 4.3, as Israel did, Psalm 106.15. We should pray in the Lord Jesus' name and ask only for things which will bring glory to the Father, John 14.13,14. We should pray at all times in the Spirit, Ephesians 6.18. The Spirit prays *for* us although we cannot always understand what He is saying. [Notice the *groaning* of .... v.22; of .... v.23; and of .... v.26.]

27. God can know everything; He knows our thoughts and our troubles even when we do not pray out loud. He also knows what the Holy Spirit wants because the Spirit is God. The Holy Spirit

prays for the *saints* of God, not only those at Rome, 1.7, but for all
who belong to Christ. The Lord Jesus also knows our thoughts,
Revelation 2.23, and prays for us, 8.34.

We cannot know the thoughts and troubles of other
Christians but we should pray for one another according
to God's will, 2 Corinthians 1.11.

28. Believers have trouble in this world, but God their Father
knows all about it. He loves His children and has all power. Why
then does He allow these things? This verse teaches that God is
working all things together for our *good*. All believers love God,
but if we love Him more we will trust Him more perfectly. We will
understand the truth of this verse and believe that God is always
working for us. We are all *called* according to His purpose.

29. What is God's great purpose? To glorify His beloved Son.
God planned long ago to make all His sons more like His Only Son,
the Lord Jesus Christ. God loved His Son before He created the
world, John 17.24. He was very well pleased with the perfect life
of His Son when He was here on earth, Matthew 3.17. God wants
us to be like Christ. This is **the good**, the best thing that could
happen to us. God works all things together for our good, that we
might be more like Christ.

God knows all things, past and future. He knew who would
be blessed in Christ and He marked them out to be made like Him.
When the Lord comes back, we will be like Him forever, so He calls
us His *brothers,* Hebrews 2.11. The word *first* does not mean created
first. The Son was never created nor born again. We are God's
creatures and had to be born again to get into God's family. We
are *brothers* because we have God's life in us, and because we act
like the Lord Jesus. Of course, the Lord Jesus is the **First** of all.
Read Colossians 1.15,18; Hebrews 1.6; Revelation 1.5.

30. Here the Holy Spirit gives us three more steps in God's
plan. God marked out long ago those He knew would be His, v.29.
He *called* them as the king called people to his great supper, Matthew 22.3,9,14; 2 Thessalonians 2.14. Then He *justified* them
through faith in Christ. Finally He gives them *glory* with Christ.
This is God's plan and He will certainly do what He has planned.
The Holy Spirit used the word *glorified* although it is still in the
future for us who are alive. God has planned it, that finishes it, it

is as good as done. But even now it is glory for us to be the sons of God, to have God as our Father.

God existed in the eternal ages of the **past** before He created anything. He knew then who would be His and He planned great blessing for us. Two things take place while we are alive at the **present** time: He calls us and justifies us. We will be with Christ in glory in the eternal ages of the **future**. This is God's plan and it cannot fail. Thank Him just now for what He is, and praise Him for what He has done for you.

In the past	In the present time	In the future
1. God knew us, v.29	1. He called us, v.30, and He justified us, v.30	1. He will give us glory with Christ, v.30
2. God planned that we should be like Christ, v.29	2. He makes things work together so we will become more like Christ, v.28	2. We shall see the Lord and be like Him forever, 1 John 3.2

Nothing can ever separate us from God's love, 8.31-39

2/29 *No enemy can stand against us, vs.31,32. No one can condemn us again, vs.33,34. No one can take us out of the love of Christ or the love of God, vs.35-39.*

31. God is working everything for our good and will certainly take us into glory. It is clear that God Almighty is our Friend, He is on our side, He cares for us and stands up for us. Who can be against us? It is true that we still have enemies in this world, but God will surely gain the victory over them for us. **32.** We can be perfectly certain that God loves us because He gave His own Son for us. God always loved His own dear Son, but He did not hold

Him back from the cross, He gave Him as a sacrifice for us. God
Himself could give no one greater. This kind of love will not refuse
to give us everything we need. *All things are yours,* 1 Corinthians
3.21.

33. Who can bring any charge against those whom God has
chosen? Satan may try to do so; he is called the accuser of the
brothers, Revelation 12.10. But God is the Judge of heaven and
earth and He has already stated that we are clear of any charge.
He will not listen to any accusation which Satan or others may
bring against us.

34. Satan may accuse us, but no one can condemn us. God
has given to Christ all authority to judge, John 5.22,27, but Christ
is the very One who died so God would not have to condemn us.
God raised Him from death which proves forever that God accepted
His sacrifice. More still, God put the Lord Jesus on His own throne
in heaven. And there He is today, our Saviour, praying for us at all
times, Hebrews 7.25. There is no condemnation for God's chosen
people, 8.1.

2/30 **35.** Even after all this someone might be afraid that he could
lose the love of Christ. Paul lists here seven kinds of trouble and he
himself had been through most of them, 2 Corinthians 11.23-27.
Many Christians in those days suffered these things and some still
do, Hebrews 10.32-34. Their enemies persecute them, steal their
food and clothing, and kill some of them. These things cannot separate us from the love of Christ: Christ loves us all the more if we
suffer for His glory. [Find seven questions in verses 31-35. Which
ones can be answered by **No** or **No one?**]

> Love for the world can keep us from loving God, 1 John
> 2.15. Trouble cannot separate us from God's love, but it
> can keep us from bearing fruit, Matthew 13.21,22.

36. The Scriptures tell us that we should expect trouble and
persecution, 1 Peter 2.21. Here the Holy Spirit used a verse from
Psalm 44.22, where men of Israel said they were in danger of being
killed all day long because they belonged to God. They were not
able to help themselves, they were like sheep which the butcher
is going to kill for meat. Many Christians have been killed just because they belong to the Lord, but this cannot separate them from
His love. In fact, they go to be with the Lord at once and this is far

better, Philippians 1.23. **37.** Anyone who hurts or kills a Christian may think that he has gained a victory, but he simply cannot separate us from Christ's love. No one can stand against us because God is on our side, v.31. The victory is ours.

> Even the little troubles of ordinary life should turn us to the Lord. We should thank God for His great love and praise Him even for the troubles, because He makes all these things work together for our good, v.28. This is true victory for the Christian.

3/1 **38,39.** So the Holy Spirit guided the apostle to list ten more things which cannot separate us from the love of God.

1,2. Death by a sword was the last thing in verse 35; here it is the first. Life may be harder and more dangerous than death for a Christian.

3,4. Some angels and other spirits fight on Satan's side and are enemies of God's people.

5,6. Nothing in the present time and nothing in the future can separate us from God.

> In the **past** our sins did indeed keep us away from God, but now the Lord Jesus Christ has removed sin by His own sacrifice for ever, Hebrews 9.26.

7. **Powers** might be wicked spirits or men; they cannot separate us from God's love even if they do miracles, 2 Thessalonians 2.9.

8,9. Nothing in space, nothing in the heavens above nor in hell below can separate us from God's love.

10. Is there anything else? The Holy Spirit said that no creature will be able to separate us from the Creator. **He** has all power, and He wants those He loves to be with Him. **Nothing, no one, can ever spoil God's plan.**

> In this chapter we have *no condemnation* in verse 1. In verses 35-39 we have *no separation*. This is the love of God which comes to us through the Lord Jesus Christ.

3/2   **TEST YOURSELF ON CHAPTER 8**

1. There is no condemnation for those who are in Christ Jesus. But how do I get into Christ?
2. Why is the Holy Spirit called the *Spirit of Life?*
3. What is the law of the Spirit?
4. In what three ways have the righteous demands of the law been fulfilled?
5. When do we get the new life and new bodies?
6. Are all children of God also *heirs* of God?
7. What will happen in Nature when the Lord comes?
8. How are we saved by *hope?*
9. Who prays for all God's people?
10. What is the greatest purpose of God? Why did He create everything, and why did He plan to redeem men?
11. What is the very best thing God can do for me?
12. What can really separate me from God's love?

Check your answers on page 140

GOD HAS HIS PLANS

FOR ISRAEL

chapters 9-11

3/3   Romans is the Good News that God saves men through faith when they believe in the Lord Jesus Christ. We are justified by the grace of God, and by the blood of Christ. No one can perfectly keep the law of God, but we are saved without it. God can save us and give us victory over sin day by day. He will soon take us to Glory to be with Himself. All this agrees with what the Bible teaches, but these truths are given more clearly in Romans.

The Old Testament is the larger part of the Bible, and most of the Old Testament is about Israel. Many people of Israel refuse to believe the Gospel because it seems to set aside both Israel and the law of God. The Holy Spirit now takes three chapters to show what God plans to do with Israel. He has never changed His own promises and never will. Some of His promises referred to true believers, chapter 9, not to the nation of Israel which had refused to accept Christ, chapter 10. However, God is going to bless the nation of Israel in a wonderful way when it turns back to Him, chapter 11.

Who are the true Israel? chapter 9

God promised great blessings for Abraham and his descendants. Who are these descendants? His sons and their sons are the natural descendants of Abraham after the flesh. All believers are the true spiritual descendants of Abraham, Galatians 3.7. Paul loved

77

his own people, vs.1-5, but the Holy Spirit shows us here who are the true Israel, vs.6-29. Why did Israel fail? The Holy Spirit begins to give the answer in vs.30-33, and continues to answer this question in chapter 10.

Paul loved his own nation, 9.1-5

Paul was a Jew, but he taught that Israel had failed to keep God's law, and no one can be saved by the law. Some Jews thought that Paul did not love his own nation, but he wrote in these verses that he would be willing to die for them if it were possible.

1. He stated very strongly that he was telling the truth. No Christian should tell a lie to anyone and certainly not to another Christian. We have seen that our conscience can help us if we know God's Word, 2.15. The Holy Spirit lived in Paul and Paul could say before God that he was speaking the truth. 2. He was very sad in his heart because most of his fellow Jews had rejected the Good News.

3. Many years before this Moses had asked the Lord to take his name out of God's book unless He could forgive Israel's sin, Exodus 32.32. Paul felt the same way, but he knew nothing could take him from Christ, 8.35-39. Moses and Paul loved the people of God, but only the Perfect Man could die for the sins of others.

4. Why did Paul love Israel so much? Because God had blessed them. Note seven blessings in this verse. They were the descendants of Israel, whose name means *prince with God,* Genesis 32.28. God named them His *sons,* not as individuals, but as a nation, Exodus 4.22. Every person must be born again to become a son of God. God showed that He was willing to live with Israel when He put the cloud of *glory* on the tabernacle, and on the temple, Exodus 40.34; 2 Chronicles 7.1. He gave Israel His covenants, His law, and His promises. Israel had the privilege of true worship, John 4.22.

5. The Israelites were descendants of Abraham, Isaac and Jacob, great men of God, but the most important thing is that the Lord Jesus Christ was an Israelite. He was far more than a great Jew. He was and is the Eternal Son of God. Here the Holy Spirit teaches these two great truths: Christ is a Man, born in the race of Israel; He is also God who is over all things and who will receive our praise forever.

Satan will admit today that Jesus is a Man, but hates the fact that He is God. Many people say that they belong to Christ, but they deny that He is the Eternal God. Even some modern Bibles make this verse sound as if Christ is only a Man, and that we should give our praise to God. The New Testament teaches in many places that Christ is the Son of God. Read again carefully John 1.1,3,14,18; Acts 9.20; Colossians 1.15-19; Hebrews 1.2-5; 1 John 1.3.

Who are the true Israel? 9.6-29

3/4 *Here the Holy Spirit answers this question by explaining God's promises to Abraham, vs.6-9. God is able to choose anyone He wishes, vs.10-18; and God's will is to show mercy, vs.19-29.*

God's promise to Abraham, 9.6-9

6,7. Of course the Word of God can never fail, we can be sure of that. But there is a great difference between the sons of Jacob and the true Israel, between the natural descendants of Abraham, and the true descendants of Abraham. Many people of Israel do not have faith in Christ, but Abraham was a man of great faith. The Holy Spirit quoted from Genesis 21.12 to prove that God's promise was not to all Abraham's natural descendants. Ishmael was a son of Abraham, but he was not a man of faith. Abraham had many other sons, Genesis 25.2,6. A true descendant of Abraham is one who is like Abraham, one who has faith in Christ, Galatians 3.9,29.

8,9. All Abraham's natural descendants are not children of God. Isaac was a man of faith, and he was born according to God's promise. God promised Abraham that his true wife Sarah would have a son, Genesis 18.10. Ishmael was born according to natural law, but it was a miracle when Isaac was born, because both Abraham and Sarah were very old, Genesis 17.17. So today God's promises are for those who have faith.

The children of Christians have many advantages, but they will not get eternal life unless they have faith. The people of Israel thought they could claim God's blessing just because they were descendants of Abraham and Isaac. If so, the descendants of Ishmael and Esau could claim the same blessing, yet these nations were the enemies of Israel.

WHO ARE THE DESCENDANTS OF ABRAHAM?

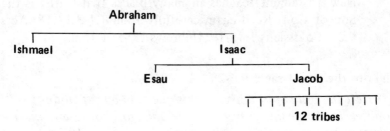

True descendants of Abraham are Jews and Gentiles who believe in Christ.

God is able to choose anyone He wishes, 9.10-18.

3/5   *God chose Jacob, and not Esau, vs.10-13. He told Moses that He would show mercy according to His own will, vs.14-16, and He raised up Pharaoh so He could show His great power, vs.17-18.*

10. God is supreme; He knows everything and He has all power. He chose Jacob rather than Esau. Both were the sons of Isaac and Rebecca; they were born together, in fact, Esau was born a few minutes before Jacob.

11,12. Before they were born, God told Rebecca that the younger son, Jacob, would be the greater man spiritually, Genesis 25.23. This proved that God chose Jacob because He wanted to, not because Jacob had done many good things and Esau was a sinner.

God chose Jacob, 9.10-13

13. Of course God knew in advance what kind of men they would be. Long after they had died, God said through His prophet that He loved Jacob and hated Esau, Malachi 1.2,3. Esau deserved to be punished, but even Jacob did nothing to make God love him.

We know that God loves all men, but He showed Malachi that He was going to punish the men of Edom who were the descendants of Esau. Still God loved every individual in the nation of Edom, and anyone who believed would have been saved.

God shows mercy according to His own will, 9.14-16

3/6 **14.** This does not mean that God is unfair to some people. God is, and always will be, righteous; this is part of His nature. Satan may accuse God of being unfair as he did when he said God showed more care for Job than for other men, Job 1.10. But this is not true. **15.** All men have sinned and no one can claim God's mercy or pity. He will show His mercy to men, but this is entirely according to His own will.

The Holy Spirit says that God spoke to Moses, Exodus 33.19. Moses wrote the book of Exodus and many times he said that God spoke to him. We can be sure that all 66 books in the true Bible are the Word of God. Some Bibles contain more than these 66 books; they have a few books which men have written by themselves.

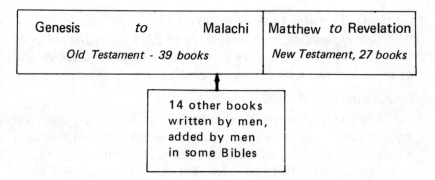

THE TRUE WORD OF GOD, 66 BOOKS

Genesis *to* Malachi	Matthew *to* Revelation
Old Testament - 39 books	*New Testament, 27 books*

14 other books
written by men,
added by men
in some Bibles

16. God's mercy depends only on Himself. I may want very much to be born again, or try very hard, like a man running in a race, but only the God of mercy can save me, John 1.13; Titus 3.5.

God raised up Pharaoh, 9.17,18

17. Pharaoh, king of Egypt, tried to keep the people of Israel from leaving his land. God gave Moses power to do many miracles, but Pharaoh would not give in. God told Pharaoh that He had made him king of Egypt so that He could show His great power to all the people of the world. The Lord could have judged Pharaoh the first time he refused to obey, but He allowed him to remain king so that all men would know that He was God. Finally God had to kill the oldest boy in every family before Pharaoh would let Israel go, Exodus 11.4,5,8. 18. So we see that God shows mercy to people according to His own will. Those who refuse His mercy become hard in their own hearts. God gave Pharaoh many opportunities to turn from his sin, but each time Pharaoh became harder.

The Bible is the Living Word of God, and it has real power. We should be very careful when we read or listen to the Bible, because it will either draw us toward God or it will make us harder. Do not think that **God** chooses some men and makes their hearts hard, so they never have an opportunity to be saved. If they harden their hearts, some day they will no longer have another opportunity. [What does the Holy Spirit tell us as believers in Hebrews 3.8, 15; 4.7?]

God's will is to show mercy, 9.19-29

3/7   *God is supreme, and over all, vs.19-21. He uses His power to show His mercy, vs.22-24. He shows His mercy to the Gentiles, and to those in Israel who believe, vs.25-29.*

God is Supreme, 9.19-21

19. The teaching of this chapter is clear, but some people will say that no one can resist God's will, and so how can God find fault with us? They think that God has refused in advance to give some men any opportunity to be saved, but this is not true. God wants all men to be saved, 1 Timothy 2.4.

20,21. No man should ask God such questions. We are like pots which God has made. A pot cannot talk back to the one who

made it, and say, *You did not make me,* or, *You were not wise,*
or, *Why did you make me like this?* Isaiah 29.16; 45.9. We should
never demand that God tell us **why**. A man can take some clay and
make two different pots of clay. He spends a lot of time to make
one pot very beautiful, but the other is a common pot which he
would use every day. God is supreme, and creatures cannot talk
back to Him.

If God were unrighteous the government of the whole
world would fall apart. No one would know what to do
next. There would be no order and everything would be
upside down. But, no, God never changes and He cannot
fail. The trouble is, men do not know Him, nor trust Him.

God uses His power to show His mercy, 9.22-24

3/8   **22.** God has a perfect right to judge sinners, and to offer them
His mercy. He could judge immediately those who sin, but He
holds back His anger for a long time. He must show all men that
He hates sin, and surely has the power to punish sinners, but He
patiently waits, although many men have already fully shown by
their sins that they are ready for God's judgment. **23.** Why does
God wait so long? He wants to make people know the great glory
that He gives to those who receive His mercy. He prepares these
believers here on earth, so they will be ready for glory in heaven.
God also shows patience because He wants all men to turn from
their sin, 2 Peter 3.9. **24.** We who believe are the objects of God's
mercy. He has called both Jews and Gentiles. He has the right to
call Gentiles, v.21, and is certainly righteous when He does so, v.14.

God shows His mercy to Gentiles and Jews, 9.25-29.

25,26. Now the Holy Spirit takes us back again to the Old
Testament, and quotes from the prophet Hosea. God had called
Israel *His people* ever since the time of Moses, Exodus 3.7,10; 19.5,
but they went on in sin until God had to say to Hosea that Israel
was **not** His people and He would not show them mercy, Hosea
1.6,9. Still, God did not completely turn from Israel and He told
the prophet that they again would be called His people, Hosea
2.23; 1.10; 1 Peter 2.10. Here we learn that God can show the
same mercy to the Gentiles. He never called the Gentiles His people,
but now He can and does. *He also calls us His beloved,* 1.7, and
His sons, 8.14.

3/9   **27.** God offered His mercy to Israel, but they refused. Still God had promised Abraham that he would have many descendants, like the little grains of sand on the sea shore, Genesis 22.17. However, God did not promise that **all** of Abraham's family would be saved, and the Holy Spirit showed Isaiah that only a small part of the nation would accept God's mercy, Isaiah 10.22,23.

28. God will fulfil His word and judge the nation of Israel because they do not accept His Son. When God's time comes, He will **suddenly** judge Israel and the whole world; men will not have another chance to turn to the Lord. Still part of Israel will believe, and this part will become very large - like the *sand by the sea shore,* Hosea 1.10.

29. Isaiah said something else, Isaiah 1.9. He said that the Lord God would leave at least a very few people in Israel who believed in Him, a small number like a *seed.* God would not destroy the whole nation if a few of them were trusting in Him. Isaiah saw that most of the people of Israel had sinned greatly against the Lord, but he knew that God would have saved even the city of Sodom if He had found only ten righteous men in it, Genesis 18.32. Most of the people of Israel were no better than the men of Sodom and Gomorrah, and they were very wicked, Jude 7; Isaiah 1.4.

Isaiah called God the *Lord of Hosts.* This name of God is found more than 260 times in the Old Testament, also in James 5.4. It means that He is Lord of all the armies of angels, Luke 2.13. These angels will punish wicked men when the Lord comes again, 2 Thessalonians 1.7,8; Revelation 15.1.

Why did Israel fail? 9.30-33

3/10   *This question is answered more fully in chapter 10, but first the Holy Spirit gives us in short form the main teaching of chapter 9.*

30. In the Old Testament the Gentiles did not seek for God, in fact, they turned **Israel** away from the Lord, Leviticus 20.23; Numbers 25.2; 1 Kings 11.1-8; Ezekiel 11.12. Now many Gentiles are made right with God because they believe the Good News. **31.** But Israel tried to earn righteousness by keeping the law. This was a great mistake and they did not succeed. **32.** They did not have faith and no one can get right with God on the ground of his own works, 3.20. The Jews did not want to believe in a Man who had been crucified, 1 Corinthians 1.23.

33. God gave His Son as the Saviour of Israel. Christ is called the *Rock,* 1 Corinthians 10.4, just as God is called the *Rock* in the Old Testament, Psalm 18.2. This name of God means that He never changes, and we can fully trust Him. But the Son of God came into the world and looked like an ordinary man. The Jews did not believe that Jesus was the Son of God, and they would not accept a Saviour who had died on a cross. To *stumble* or *trip* means to refuse to believe because you do not understand. God sent His Son to Zion, or Jerusalem, and many Jews refused Him. Those who believe in Christ will never be disappointed.

In Isaiah 8.14, the Lord is a *stumbling* stone, Matthew 21.44, but in Isaiah 28.16, He is a *precious* stone, 1 Peter 2.7. If you love the Lord, say a little word of thanks to Him right now.

3/11 **TEST YOURSELF ON CHAPTER 9**

1. Could Paul put himself under God's curse to save his own people Israel?
2. Write out the special blessings of Israel, using the words of your own Bible in verse 4.
3. What does verse 5 teach about the God-Man, our Lord Jesus Christ?
4. God gave wonderful promises to the descendants of Abraham. How is He going to fulfil these promises?
5. Did God really hate Esau?
6. God knows in advance all who will be saved. Does this mean that no others can be saved?
7. Did Pharaoh have any opportunity to be saved?
8. God does not judge men at once when they sin. Why?
9. God now called Gentiles *His people.* What else does He call those who believe?
10. Why did God reject Israel?
11. Why does the Holy Spirit call God the *Lord of Hosts?*
12. Why does the Holy Spirit call God *the Rock?*

Check your answers on page 141

Israel's failure and our responsibility, chapter 10

3/12   We have seen that God's plans never fail, but only a part of Israel will be saved. The Spirit now explains more fully why Israel as a nation cannot claim God's full blessing. In chapter 10 we have two ways to get right with God, vs.1-13. Then we will see that we must tell people how they can be saved, but they must believe the message, vs.14-21.

Righteousness, 10.1-13

Israel tried to earn righteousness by keeping the law of Moses, vs.1-4, but now God has told us plainly how to be saved, vs.5-13.

Righteousness by law, 10.1-4

1. Paul could have wished that he might be under the curse for Israel's sake, 9.1-3. He wanted more than anything else to see his own people Israel saved, and he prayed to God to grant this. **2.** Before Paul was saved, he was very devoted to God, Acts 22.3. He knew that many Jews were also devoted to Him, but they did not know God's truth fully. **3.** They did not know that God is **perfectly** righteous. If they had known they would not have tried to make themselves righteous. God is so righteous that He **must** punish sin. He cannot pass lightly over a man's sins just because the man tries to keep the law and do a few good works.

It is God's special privilege to justify the sinner, and we must never try to set up our **own** righteousness.

4. Christ is the *end* of the law. He perfectly obeyed the law; He bore the punishment of the law when He died for all men. Therefore God can righteously justify everyone who believes in Christ.

Righteousness by faith, 10.5-13

3/13   **5.** The law is a way to get life, for anyone who can perfectly fulfil every command, Leviticus 18.5; Romans 7.10. **6.** People who have failed are glad to hear about another way to get righteousness. They do not have to go very far to learn God's way of righteousness. Someone might say, "We must go to heaven before we can know", but Christ has already come from heaven to tell us God's way, John 3.12,13. We cannot ask Him to come back to tell us again.

7. Another person might say that we can ask those who have already died; or, we cannot have righteousness until we have died. But our Lord Jesus Christ has died, and has risen from death. We can receive God's righteousness here and now, and we can know we have it. **8.** We know the way to be saved; Paul and all the apostles preached this Word, we have learned it, believed it and received it into our hearts. It is on our lips and we are ready to tell others also.

In the Old Testament, Moses told Israel that they knew God's commands because he had plainly taught them, Deuteronomy 30.11-14. Here Paul used almost the same words to show that the way of salvation is easily known. We should therefore be able to understand, and to tell others.

9. What is this simple message from God? God promised in this verse that anyone can be saved, **if** he will confess openly that Jesus is his Lord, and **if** he really believes that God raised Him from the dead. Why are these two things so important? God raised Christ from death; this shows that Christ died and God approved of His sacrifice on the cross. I really believe this in my heart, and so I accept Christ as my Saviour, Acts 16.31. At the same time I accept Him as my **Lord,** and give Him control of my life. This also is real, and I must let other people know that Christ is my Lord.

Some people try to hide this so that others will not laugh at them or hate them. But this means they have to keep on committing sin, and if they do, they are not being saved from the power of sin. We have seen that God can save us from the penalty of sin, 3.21 - 5.21, and He can keep us from sinning, chapters 6-8. We need the power of the Holy Spirit to help us say that Jesus is Lord, 1 Corinthians 12.3.

3/14   **10.** This verse teaches the same two truths, but in the opposite order. In verse 9, the first truth is that Christ is Lord, and the second that He rose from death. The Son of God always was Lord, but He became a Man, He died and rose again. But as a sinner, I believe first, and then I confess Christ as Lord; so in verse 10 we see our own experience. The *heart* is what I really am inside, but the *lips* show this to others.

There is a difference between the words *justified* and *saved*.

God does both of these things to any sinner when he believes on the Lord Jesus Christ. We have seen that God puts the sinner on new ground when He justifies him. God, the righteous Judge, declares to all persons that Christ has paid the price for my sin, and I will never again be considered a guilty sinner. I am justified.

As Saviour, God saves me from the penalty of sin **and** also from the power of sin. This means that He has forgiven all my sins and will help me by the Holy Spirit to obey the Lord. He saves me and keeps on saving me every day.

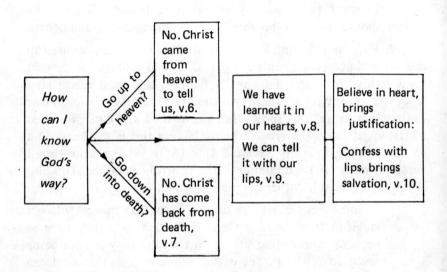

11. Any living person can believe and be saved. The Holy Spirit here used again the same verse as He did in 9.33. Those who trust in themselves will be disappointed; all who trust in Christ will certainly be saved.

If God says a thing, all men should listen and obey. If He says the same thing two or three times, it must be very important. Here in Romans 9.33 and 10.11 the Holy Spirit used the words of Isaiah 28.16, but changed them a little.

The Holy Spirit is the Author of the Old Testament and He
has the right to change His own words when He wants to.

12. Jews have many advantages, 3.1; 9.4,5; 10.2, but they
are just as guilty before God as the Gentiles, 3.22,23. God is the
God of all men, 3.29; He calls both Jews and Gentiles, 9.24, and is
Lord of all, 10.12. He is *rich* and can supply all the sinner needs, if
he calls on the Lord for help. **13.** Again the Holy Spirit quotes
from the Old Testament, this time from Joel 2.32. *Everyone who
calls on the Lord will be saved.* Peter used this verse when he was
speaking to the people in Jerusalem on the day of Pentecost,
Acts 2.21.

> God has authority to make men according to His own
> will, 9.21, but here He offers salvation to all. Of course, it
> is not enough just to **say** the name of the Lord Jesus; it
> must be real and from the heart, v.11; Matthew 7.21-23;
> 25.11,12.

Responsibility, 10.14-21

3/15 *So people must call on the Lord if they want to be saved. Now
we learn that our duty is to tell all men about the Lord, vs.14-17,
but they must believe to get the blessing, vs.18-21.*

14,15. First Paul by the Holy Spirit asked four questions beginning with the word *How*. (Write down your answer to each
question.)

1. How can anyone really call on Christ to save him unless he
   believes in Christ as his Saviour? _____

2. How can anyone believe in Christ if he never even heard
   about him? _____

3. How can anyone hear unless someone tells him the message?
   _____

4. How can anyone go with the message unless he is sent?
   _____

You see that people must believe before they can be saved,
and we must tell them about Christ before they can believe. The
Lord Jesus has certainly told us to preach the Good News, Matthew
28.19; Mark 16.15; Luke 24.48; John 20.21; Acts 1.8. The Holy
Spirit told the church at Antioch to send out Paul and Barnabas
because He had called them to preach the Good News in other

lands, Acts 13.2. Here in verse 15 the Holy Spirit quoted part of
Isaiah 52.7. A messenger uses his feet to go and deliver his message.
If he brings good news he is most welcome, and even his feet seem
to be beautiful.

Isaiah spoke of one Person, the Lord Jesus Christ, God's
Messenger, who brought the Good News of God's love. But
here the Holy Spirit speaks of **many** believers who have
the honour of doing the same work as Christ did, 2 Corinthians 5.18. New Testament churches should pray about
sending out young men and young women to tell others
the Good News.

16. We must keep on preaching the Good News, even if many
people do not believe. Isaiah had asked God if **anyone** believed his
message. God knows those who believe, but Isaiah could hardly
find even one, Isaiah 53.1; John 12.38.

The Lord had warned Isaiah that most of the people
would not believe what he taught, Isaiah 6.9-12. The Lord
told Jeremiah and Ezekiel almost the same thing, Jeremiah
1.17-19; Ezekiel 3.4,7. We should not give up, even though
we do not see many people turning to the Lord.

17. The Holy Spirit states again in a few words the main
lessons of verses 14-16. Some people may believe the message and
some reject it, but no one can believe until he has heard. Two
things are necessary for blessing: we must tell people about Christ
and they must believe the message.

3/16   18. We have failed to tell all people the Good News, but still
they can learn something about God if they just consider the world
around them. David by the Holy Spirit taught that the stars and
the sun declared God's glory, and all men everywhere could understand, Psalm 19.1-4. Paul taught the same truth, Romans 1.19,20.
Men are guilty before God because they do not try to please the
One who created them.

Nature tells men that God is wise and powerful, but the
Lord has commanded us to tell them about His **love**.

19. The Jews certainly had the truth of God, and should have
known that He would save the Gentiles who believed. The apostle
Paul quoted from Deuteronomy 32.21, which was written by Moses.

Israel made God angry when they worshipped other gods and so God made them jealous when He gave great blessing to other nations.

20. Isaiah spoke more strongly still when he said that Gentile nations would find God even though they had not been seeking Him, Isaiah 65.1. The Jews hated this teaching, but God gave Isaiah courage to speak His word. **21.** God expected Israel to tell all men about His love and righteousness, but they never obeyed Him. They worshipped idols and broke God's law. He appealed to them like a man holding out his hands, but they rebelled and refused to listen.

The prophet Jonah was an example of the whole nation of Israel. God commanded Jonah to go to the great Gentile city of Nineveh and warn the people there that He would judge them. The prophet tried to run away, but God brought him back. Jonah warned the people of Nineveh, and they repented, but he seemed to be sorry that God did not judge them, Jonah 1.2,3; 3.1-3,10; 4.1. Israel never really took the truth of God to the Gentile nations.

Has the Church done better than Israel? The Lord told us to witness to Him in every country, and Paul could say that the Christians had preached the Good News in his days in the whole world, Colossians 1.6,23. But it has never happened again since the time of Paul. Today there are millions of people who have never heard about the name of the Lord Jesus or the love of God. If they do not hear, they cannot believe the Good News.

3/17 **TEST YOURSELF ON CHAPTER 10**

1. Israel thought they knew the truth of God. Were they right in thinking this?
2. How was Christ the *end* of the law?
3. People want to know the way to be saved. Do they need to go up to heaven, or down into death?
4. Why is it necessary to confess Christ in order to be saved?
5. Why does verse 10 use a different order than verse 9, putting *believing* before *declaring*?
6. Was I saved **before** I was justified, or **after**?
7. Where in the New Testament does the Holy Spirit use words from Isaiah 28.16? .... ; from Joel 2.32? .... ; from Isaiah 53.1? ....

8. What do **we** have to do before people can believe in Christ?
9. Even before we tell them, how could they know about God?
10. Why did God make Israel jealous?
11. Why was Jonah unhappy when the men of Nineveh turned from their sins?

Check your answers on pages 141, 142

God will bless the true Israel, chapter 11

3/18 We have seen that God's promises cannot change, and that there will be many true believers in Israel, chapter 9. The nation has failed because they thought they could get righteousness by keeping the law, yet they did not really obey God, 10.3,21. Now we will learn about Israel's condition at the present time, vs.1-10; God's eternal plan, vs.11-24; and the future blessing of the Jews, vs.25-32. At the end of the chapter Paul praised God for His great wisdom and power.

What is Israel's condition at the present time? 11.1-10

Israel has rejected the Lord Jesus and so God has rejected them, but not the **whole** *nation, vs.1-4. There is a small group in Israel who are saved by grace, vs.5,6, but most of the people are blind, vs.7-10.*

1. The strong language of Isaiah might make you think that God has completely rejected His people, Israel, but this is not true. Paul himself was a descendant of Abraham, Israel and Benjamin. Paul was a true believer, and there were other Jews who believed in Christ, some of them in the assembly in Rome.

2-4. God knew long ago what Israel would do even before He chose them. Most of them disobeyed Him, but He has not changed His mind. The prophet Elijah loved the Lord and felt very badly when Israel departed from God. He prayed God and asked Him to judge Israel so they would return to the Lord. God had said He would not send rain and people would go hungry if they did not keep His laws, Deuteronomy 28.23,24. Elijah prayed for three and a half years that God would not send rain, and at last the people did return to Jehovah, 1 Kings 17.1; 18.39; James 5.17,18. Even then Elijah knew that the wicked Queen Jezebel was trying to kill him. Elijah thought that he was the only one left in the land who believed in Jehovah, but God said there were **7,000** who had never worshipped the idols of Baal, 1 Kings 19.2,10,18.

5,6. Paul knew that there was a small remnant of Israel in his time who did believe the Good News. God chose these in His *mercy*. This shows again that God saves men because of His grace and not because of their works.

> These two ideas of grace and works are opposites, Ephesians 2.8,9. God's grace, mixed with our works, does not bring glory to God, and is no longer pure grace. If I work for my own salvation, then I am trying to pay God for what He wants to give me.

3/19 **7.** The nation of Israel tried to get righteousness, 9.31, but most of them failed because they did not understand God's ways, 10.3. But some in Israel did believe in the Lord Jesus Christ, and God chose them for blessing. He hardened the hearts of the rest as He had hardened Pharaoh, 9.17,18.

8. Long before this, Moses and Isaiah by the Holy Spirit said that God had given the sinners of Israel minds that were not sharp, eyes that did not see, and ears which could not hear, Deuteronomy 29.4; Isaiah 6.9,10; 29.10. These people could see everything around them, and hear what others said, but they could not understand God's message to them. This was because they did not want to obey God. [Which verses in Isaiah did the Lord Jesus use in Matthew 13.14,15?]

9,10. David used stronger language still when he asked God to judge his enemies, who were really the enemies of God, Psalm 69.22. People usually eat feasts at a *table* with their family and

friends. God has invited us to be happy with Him, Psalm 23.5;
Matthew 22.4; Revelation 3.20. David prayed against the sinners
of Israel as Elijah did, v.2. David asked God that Israel might not
get His blessing. He prayed that they might not see His glory, but
might bend their backs like slaves who have to work very hard.

God's eternal plan, 11.11-24

3/20 *God has all power and He does not have to tell men what He
is going to do, but He loves us as sons, and wants us to know His
plans and His reasons, John 15.15. We can understand why He set
Israel to one side when we see that He wants to bring great blessing
on the Gentiles, vs.11-16. Indeed even now the Jews reject the
Good News but it goes out to all nations, vs.17-22. In the future,
God will again turn and bless Israel, vs.23,24.*

God will bless Gentiles through Israel, 11.11-16

11. The nation of Israel has fallen, but not completely: some
are being saved, and in the future all the Jews who are alive will
turn to the Lord. God wants Jews who are living now to return to
their Messiah, the Lord Jesus. The Jews see many Gentiles getting
the blessing of Abraham; this should make them jealous and want
to get the blessing for themselves, 10.19.

12. The nation of Israel has fallen into sin and this has resulted in spiritual riches for Gentiles, because the Good News has
gone out to them. God will put Israel again in the place of full
favour and this will mean still more blessing for all other men.

13,14. Most of the Christians at Rome were Gentiles, and
Paul was an apostle whom the Lord had sent especially to the
Gentiles, Acts 9.15; 22.21; Romans 15.16. Paul was very happy
to obey his Lord and tell Gentiles about all their blessings in
Christ. Still he hoped and prayed that many of his own nation
would turn to God.

How could Paul *save* anyone since Christ is the only
Saviour? Paul could help people to get saved by telling
them about the Saviour, and warning them to turn from
their sins, 1 Corinthians 9.22. A man may *save* his wife,
and a woman may *save* her husband, in the same way, 1 Corinthians 7.16. We should always live for Christ and tell
others about Him.

15. God rejected Israel and sent out the wonderful message that He loves all men, and wants them to be His friends. Israel as a nation is now far from God, so is *dead,* but when the time comes God will give life again to the nation which He chose long ago.

3/21 **16.** God commanded His people to bring Him the first part of every crop as soon as it was ripe, Leviticus 23.10. They should also bring a small part of the bread which they baked, Numbers 15.21; Nehemiah 10.37. This showed that everything they had belonged to the Lord. Here the apostle is speaking of Abraham whom God chose for Himself. Abraham was the first part and the root; Israel is the main part and the tree. God will bring Israel back to Himself some day still in the future.

God is blessing Gentiles even now, 11.17-22

17,18. Some people are expert at gardening and can take the branch of one tree and attach it to another. If the two trees are alike, the new branch will grow and bear fruit. Here Paul says the Gentiles are like a branch of a wild olive tree, and Israel is like an olive tree which God has cared for in every way. Still many Jews

did not believe and so God has broken off some of the tree's branches. God has taken Gentiles and brought them into the blessings of Abraham. We Gentiles must not think we are any better than Jews. After all, a branch can do nothing unless it is attached to a root, John 15.4. The Son of God gives His blessing to both Jew and Gentile, to all who believe and accept Him.

3/22. **19,20.** It is true that Israel has been rejected, and Gentiles have been brought into blessing. We must remember that God rejected Israel because they did not believe; we get the blessing if we believe, so there is no reason for being proud, 3.27. **21.** God punished Israel because they did not believe; He will do the same to Gentiles.

This means that God will take away our opportunity for blessing. It refers to nations, and ages of time, not to individuals. Anyone who comes to Christ will never be cut off or put out, John 6.37. But in Old Testament days God dealt with the nation of Israel and Israel failed. Now the Good News goes out to Gentiles, but the Church has failed. Soon the Lord Jesus will come back, and God will show His grace and mercy to His chosen people Israel once again.

3/23 **22.** We learn from these things that God is both kind and severe: kind to those who accept His mercy, severe to those who reject His Son. *Severe* means that God is righteous, and not that He is cruel. We must keep on trusting Him, and believing in His kindness; if not, He will punish us. We may think He is cruel, but really He punishes us to bring us back to Himself, so this proves that He loves us.

God will bless any Jew right now if he believes, 11.23,24

23. God has not finally rejected the Jews. If they turn back to Him He will receive them, and put them again in the place of blessing, like a gardener who can put a branch back into a tree after he has cut it off. God is able to do this for every Jew who believes. **24.** We were like branches of a wild olive tree; we had no part in God's covenant with Abraham, Ephesians 2.12. By His grace, God has brought us into a place of great blessing, but not because of what we are by nature. God is able to bring back the children of Israel and return them to their own place of blessing. God wants to do this, He is doing it today for individual Jews; He will do it for the nation of Israel when the Lord comes back again.

The future blessing of the Jews, 11.25-32

3/24   *God has promised to save Israel later on, vs.25-27, and He will not break His promise, vs.28,29. He will have mercy on Gentiles and Jews, vs.30-32.*

25. Paul knew what men's hearts are like: they may become proud at any time. He also knew that God cannot bless people who are proud, James 4.6; 1 Peter 5.5. We Gentiles must not think we are better or know more than the Jews. God has set Israel aside, but only part of the nation, and only for a certain time. We have seen that many Jews were saved in Paul's time, v.17, but during this age most of the people of Israel are *blind*; they refuse to believe the truth of God, and their hearts are hard. The Good News is going out to the Gentiles, and when the number of Gentiles is complete, God will bring back the nation of Israel into His favour.

26,27. Then *all Israel will be saved.* Of course, God will not force unbelieving Jews to come to Him. No one can ever be saved without faith. Many Jews will be killed in the terrible tribulation just before the Lord comes back in power. The living Jews will see the Lord Jesus, Zechariah 12.10; John 19.37, and will be very sorry that their nation put Him on the cross. Here Paul quoted from Isaiah 59.20,21 and 27.9. The Saviour, the Lord Jesus, will come to Mount Zion in Jerusalem and go out to all Jacob or Israel and take away their sins. God has promised to make a new covenant with His people, and never remember their sins again, Jeremiah 31.33.

28. The Good News is going out to Gentiles because the Jews have rejected it. The Jews tried to stop Paul from preaching God's message to others. They opposed God's plans, and made themselves enemies of the Gospel, 1 Thessalonians 2.15. Still God had chosen Abraham and Israel; He loved Israel, and so should we. A few Israelites believed in Paul's day; a few believe today, many will in the future. **29.** God is always the same, 1 Samuel 15.29; Malachi 3.6. He has given great privileges to Israel, 9.4,5; He will not take back His gifts. He has called Israel; He will not forget His promise.

God changes His attitude toward men when they change their attitude toward Him, for example, Genesis 6.6; 1 Samuel 15.11, but He will never change His promises, Hebrews 6.18.

3/25   **30,31.** God treats Jews and Gentiles in the same way, but
shows them mercy at different times:
>   1) The Gentiles disobeyed God in the past.
>   2) Because the Jews now disobey, God is sending the Good
>   News to the Gentiles,
>   3) and the Gentiles receive His mercy.
>   1. The Jews disobey now.
>   2. God is showing mercy to the Gentiles.
>   3. The Jews will receive God's blessing on the same
>   ground as any Gentile: because of God's mercy.

Romans 11.30,31	PAST	PRESENT	FUTURE
JEWS		disobey	will receive mercy
GENTILES	disobeyed	receive mercy	

We Gentiles should show mercy to the Jews because God certainly will. His mercy is the only reason He will bless anyone. **32.**
God controls all things so men will see that they are sinners, and
ask for His mercy. No man can save himself by good works, but
God wants to have mercy on all men. Today many people have
never heard about God's mercy, and millions who have heard
reject it.

Praise God for His great wisdom and power, 11.33-36

3/26   *God has given men the right and privilege and duty to choose
what is good and refuse what is evil. He never forces an individual
to accept Christ as Saviour. But He does control great movements
of men and nations. He does this so He can show His mercy to all
who will accept it. The Holy Spirit gave Paul these wonderful
truths and now Paul praises God for His wisdom and power. No
one can show God a better way to do things, because everything
comes from Him, and exists for His glory.*

33. No one can know all about God's riches, or His wisdom, or His knowledge. God's decisions are far wiser than any man's, and we cannot understand His ways unless He explains them to us. **34.** To prove this, Paul quoted Isaiah 40.13,14, as he did again in 1 Corinthians 2.16. We can know the way the Lord thinks only if He tells us, and He does not need any man's advice.

> The Lord has promised to answer our prayers, but this does not mean that we can tell God how to rule the world. We should always pray as the Lord Jesus Himself did, *Not what I want but what you want,* Matthew 26.39. We should also praise God for what He is, and for what He gives us, Matthew 11.25; John 11.41.

35. We have read that God is rich in mercy, and well able to save all that call upon Him, 2.4; 10.12. No one can give something **first** to God, because He gave us life when we were born, Acts 17.25. God will not accept our good works and pay us with eternal life. He gives us eternal life as a gift, 6.23, and then we can serve Him well.

36. All things came from God, and He created everything. He did it all *for* His own pleasure and glory, and Paul calls us to give Him glory for ever.

Some of these words are also used of our Lord Jesus Christ, the Son of God. Read carefully 1 Corinthians 8.6; Colossians 1.16; Revelation 4.11. The Son upholds the world by His power, Hebrews 1.3.

Stop here and praise God for all the wonderful truths of this book of Romans, and for all that He is, and for all that He has done for you.

3/27 **TEST YOURSELF ON CHAPTER 11**
1. Did Isaiah believe that God had rejected all Israel?
2. Why did Elijah think he was the only true believer left in Israel?
3. Why did David pray that God would judge his enemies?
4. Give three verses which speak of men feasting with God.
5. Will all Jewish people be saved?
6. How can Israel's sin bring blessing to Gentiles?

7. Abraham was the *root* and Israel the *branches,* v.16. What does it mean *the branches belong to God?*

8. God has broken off some of the branches and put us Gentiles into the tree of His blessing. Does this show that He loves us more than He loves Israel?

9. God is *severe,* v.22. Does this mean that He is cruel?

10. When will God put the natural branches back into the tree of blessing?

11. God is now showing His mercy especially to the Gentiles. Does this mean no Jew can be saved?

12. Why did the Lord Jesus praise His Father? Matthew 11.25.

Check your answers on page 142

GOD WANTS US
TO LIVE
A HOLY LIFE

chapters 12-15

3/28   Many books in the Bible tell us about God's Good News, but no book explains the Gospel more fully than the letter to the Romans. We have seen that God is righteous when He declares that all men, Jews and Gentiles, are guilty before Him. He remains righteous when He justifies those who believe in Christ. This is possible because Christ died for us, **not** because we have kept the law, been baptized, or done many good works. We are saved when we believe on Christ, and confess Him as Lord, 10.9.

In Romans 12-15, the Lord tells us what to do now that we are His. We were slaves to sin, 6.17; now we gladly follow our new Master. We could not keep God's law perfectly; now the Holy Spirit helps us to fulfil the law, 8.4. In these four chapters we will see how we should behave:

1. in relation to God and our brothers, chapter 12
2. in relation to the world, chapter 13
3. in relation to a weak brother, 14.1 - 15.7
4. in relation to all men, 15.8-33

Paul also wrote about his own work and plans in chapter 15.

How we should act toward God and men, chapter 12

The most important thing is to be right with God, and to do His will, vs.1,2. God loves all men, and His will is that we should do good to others. Here the Holy Spirit tells us how to behave with other believers, vs.3-13; and with all men, vs.14-21.

101

We should know and do the will of God, 12.1, 2

1. The first eleven chapters of Romans teach us that God is rich in mercy to all who will accept it. What can we now do for Him? We belong to God and we should offer ourselves wholly to Him. Both Jews and Gentiles offered up dead animal sacrifices, but Christians should offer themselves as *living* sacrifices. This means that we should live all the time for God's glory, and not try to please ourselves, 6.19.

> 1) This is necessary if we are really going to worship God.
>
> 2) We will please God if we are living clean, holy lives.
>
> 3) If we stop to think about it, we will see that this is the proper, spiritual sacrifice we should make.

2. We belong to God, not to this world, 1 John 2.15. We should not try to live and act like all the people around us. We will be able to live holy lives for God if we let Him change our hearts and give us thoughts like His own. Then we will know His will, and what He wants us to do. We will know that only God's will is really good for us. This will please Him, and it is perfect for us.

We should help other Christians, 12.3-13

3/29   *Every Christian has something to do in the assembly (the local church), verses 3-8. We should be kind to other believers, and happy in the Lord, vs. 9-13.*

In the assembly, 12.3-8

3. Paul knew that he had been saved only by the grace of God, and he had nothing to be proud of, 1 Corinthians 15.9,10. God also by grace made Paul an apostle, and so he had authority to tell the Christians to do God's will, 1.5. We also are sinners, and know we have nothing except what God has given us. God gives gifts to all believers. These gifts are given so we can help other believers, not to make us proud. It is a sin to be proud, and nothing will spoil an assembly or local church more quickly than the sin of pride. God may give greater gifts to those who have more faith.

Some Christians are not at all proud, in fact, they say they have no gift, and therefore think they cannot help in the church. This is bad because everyone is needed in the assembly. Verse 3 says that we should not think that we are *better* than we really are, but we should understand what gift God has given us and use it for His glory, and to help in the church.

4,5. The whole Church includes all living people who belong to Christ; it is called the Body of Christ, Ephesians 1.23. The local church is also like a body: Christ is the Head, and all the Christians are like the different members of the body. Each part of your body has something to do which helps the whole body. It is the same in the church, 1 Corinthians 12.12,27. The Holy Spirit lives in every Christian, and He makes us into one Body. Christ gives us instructions through the Bible. [What happens to the church when every believer does his work properly, Ephesians 4.16?]

6-8. We all have different gifts which the Holy Spirit has given us, 1 Corinthians 12.11, and we should each use our gift to help the whole church. Here Paul listed seven different gifts and tells us we should do *well* what the Spirit gives us to do.

1. The prophets in the Old Testament told the people what God wanted them to do and what **He** was going to do. There were prophets in the early church also who could tell what would happen in the future, Acts 11.27,28; 21.10,11. In those days only part of the New Testament had been written, but now it is complete. We do not have true prophets today, 1 Corinthians 13.8-10, but we have men who preach the Word. The preacher should serve the Lord fully according to his faith, but not try to go beyond what God has given him.

2. Some can *serve* the Lord's people. Any service in the assembly should be done as a service to the Lord.

3. Some have the gift of *teaching;* they must teach the Bible to others.

4. Some can give a little word of comfort to those who are sorrowful; or encourage people to follow the Lord.

5. We can all give to the Lord, but some can give more than others. They should give simply and with all their heart, Matthew 6.1.

6. Leaders must be willing to work hard in the assembly, 1 Thessalonians 5.12.

7. Some have the gift of helping those who are in trouble; they should do it cheerfully, 2 Corinthians 9.7.

There are other gifts in the assembly, 1 Corinthians 12.8-
10; Ephesians 4.11. Every believer should ask the Lord
what his gift is, then use it for the Lord and for His people.

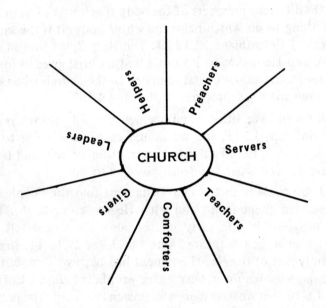

Everyone helps all others in the assembly;
no one is better than the rest, 12.3-8.

Love and joy, 12.9-13

3/30   *The Holy Spirit tells us here we should have true love and joy
in our hearts.*

9. Sometimes people can cover up hate by acting as if they
love you. Judas kissed the Lord Jesus, but it was a sign to his enemies, Matthew 26.48. Still true love does not mean that we should
let a brother go on in sin. God hates all that is evil and we should
tell another Christian if we see that he has committed a sin, Matthew 18.15. True love will also lead us to hold on to all that is good.
We must never give up any great truth just because people bring
some new teaching.

10. We will read more about love in 13.8-10. Here we should remember that God is our Father, and we are all brothers in His family. We should love one another as brothers, not like Cain who killed his brother Abel; or Esau who wanted to kill Jacob, 1 John 3.12; Genesis 27.41. We should also show respect for other Christians, and not talk about them in a bad way, as David's brother talked about him, 1 Samuel 17.28. Some people in Corinth said things against Paul which were not true, 2 Corinthians 10.10.

11. No Christian should be lazy in his daily work, and especially in his Christian work. We are servants of the Lord and should do everything for His glory. 12. Our hope is the Lord Himself, Colossians 1.27. We know He is coming back for us, and this makes us very happy. It also helps us to be patient when we have a lot of trouble, 5.3-5. But we need to ask the Lord every day to keep us patient and happy in Himself. We should keep on praying, Philippians 4.6.

13. Some Christians have the gift of helping poor believers, v.8, but we all should be ready to share what we have with other Christians who need help. We should be willing to give visitors a place to sleep, and to share our food with strangers, Hebrews 13.2; 1 Peter 4.9. This is a special command to leaders in the assembly, 1 Timothy 3.2; Titus 1.8.

We should be kind to all men, 12.14-21

4/1 *The Christian must live in this world, and the Holy Spirit tells us how we should act toward others.*

14. The Lord warned us that we can expect trouble in the world, but He promised to help us, John 16.33. He Himself did not curse His enemies, He asked God to forgive them, Luke 23.34. [What did Stephen say when the Jews were killing him, Acts 7.60?] The Holy Spirit will help us to bless our enemies.

15. We should be symphathetic to others and try to understand their problems, and share their troubles and their joys with them. This will help us to tell them that Christ is the answer to every problem, and He alone can give true joy which will last forever. Paul shared in the trials of God's people, 2 Corinthians 11.29, and so did the Lord Jesus Christ, John 11.35.

16. We should truly love other people and live in peace and

harmony with them. This means that we should not fight and quarrel with others, 2 Corinthians 13.11; Philippians 2.2; 4.2. Most quarrels are caused by pride, Proverbs 13.10. We should be friends with common people, and be willing to do humble duties. These things will not make us proud, but anyone who thinks he is wise will become proud.

4/2   **17.** All men want to hurt those who hurt them, for example, Lamech killed the young man who had wounded him, Genesis 4.23. Absalom killed his brother Amnon for attacking their sister Tamar, 2 Samuel 13.22-32. The Christian should never try to pay back anyone who has done wrong to him, Matthew 5.39. Instead we should plan to do what all men believe is good. This is so they will not have any ground for blaming us, 2 Corinthians 8.21; 1 Peter 2.12.

Of course we cannot follow the world and do what is wrong, even if everyone else says it is good. We must go by God's Word and not by men's opinions.

18-21. We should try to live at peace with all men, not get into fights or arguments. However, some people will try to start a fight and we sometimes have to stand up for the Truth, Jude 3. **19.** Now the Holy Spirit teaches us more about taking revenge. We should always wait for our God to punish those who do wrong to us. First the Spirit quoted from Deuteronomy 32.35 (as He did again in Hebrews 10.30). God has promised to look after His people and to punish those who do wrong to any believer. **20.** Then the Spirit quoted from Proverbs 25.21,22, and tells us to be kind to an enemy if he needs help. This will make him feel ashamed of the evil things he did to us; it will be like having hot coals on his head. **21.** Sometimes a believer will try to pay back an enemy and do something bad to him. This means that *evil* is winning a victory. Instead we should return good for evil; in that way what is good wins the victory.

This chapter teaches that we should give ourselves to God. In the assembly each one should serve others, according to the gift God has given him, and love others. In the world we should also show our love to men and return good for evil.

4/3 **TEST YOURSELF ON CHAPTER 12**

1. Which two verses are the most important in chapter 12? Why?
2. What is the best offering to God?
3. Why does God give gifts to believers?
4. Who are God's prophets today?
5. What should I do if I really love another Christian and he falls into some sin?
6. Why should a Christian work hard at his daily job?
7. How can I forgive a man who curses me?
8. If Christians become proud, what will happen in the assembly?

Check your answers on pages 142, 143

How we should act in relation to the world, chapter 13

4/4   We have seen that the believer should be kind to all men, 12.14-21. Now we learn that the believer should obey the government, 13.1-7, and love his neighbour, vs.8-14.

Obey the government, 13.1-7

The government gets its authority from God, vs.1,2, and should use this authority to keep peace, vs.3-5; and to collect taxes, vs.6,7.

. **1.** Every Christian should obey the government because God has all authority, and He has set up government to keep good order in the world. God has commanded men to govern themselves ever since the time of Noah: anyone who killed a man should be put to death by other men, Genesis 9.6. **2.** This means that we should not resist the authority of the government because God has commanded us to obey, and the government has the authority to punish those who disobey. **3.** People who do wrong should be afraid of the government, but rulers will praise those who do what is right.

4. We should think of people in authority as the servants of God. They help to keep peace in the state, and this is good. We do not need to be afraid of them if we obey the laws; but if not, they have authority to punish us. The *sword* is a picture of the ruler's authority. **5.** We should obey the rulers because they have authority from God to punish those who do wrong. We should also obey the law if we want to have a good conscience. [What did Paul tell Titus to teach about the government? Titus 3.1. What did Peter say we should do? 1 Peter 2.13,14.]

The conscience is that small voice in our hearts telling us to do what is right, 2.15; 9.1. The conscience speaks even when no person can see what we are doing. Because of conscience we should obey the law even when no officer is near.

4/5   **6.** Christians must be honest and pay all government taxes. These taxes make it possible for the authorities to do their work. **7.** This rule applies to all different kinds of taxes. We should also show proper respect for the authorities. Christians are not free to say whatever they like about government officials.

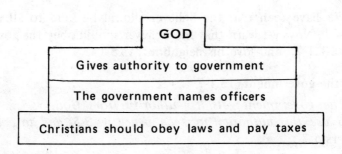

Paul always tried to have a good conscience, and to show honour to those in authority, Acts 23.1,5. The Lord Jesus also paid a tax and taught that we should pay taxes, Matthew 17.24,25; 22.17-21. The Lord also showed respect for the high priest even though Caiaphas was a wicked man, Matthew 26.63,64. In some countries today wicked men control the government. Should a Christian obey such people? Yes, God wants us to obey. However, the time may come when some government officer will tell you to worship an idol or commit a sin. Then you can remember the words of Peter, that we should obey God rather than men, Acts 4.19. Some day soon the Lord Jesus will come back to rule the whole world. Then all men will have a good and righteous government, but not before then.

Love your neighbour, 13.8-14

4/6   *We should sincerely love other people, and if we do, we fulfil the law of God. The Lord is coming soon, and we should behave as He would want us to.*

8. We should pay the government what we owe, and we should pay our debts to other people also. It is not good for a Christian to keep on owing money to others. However, one debt is to love all men; we can never finish paying this debt. The Lord Jesus taught that we should love God and men, Matthew 22.37-39. The whole law is contained in these two commands. 9. Here the Holy Spirit quoted four of the Ten Commandments, which tell us we should not do anything wrong to others. 10. If I love my neighbour, I will try to do something good for him. This is to fulfil the real meaning of the law, 8.4; it is possible in the power of the Holy Spirit. Someone will say, "Who is my neighbour?" The Lord Jesus taught that anyone I can help is my neighbour, Luke 10.29-37.

Paul felt that he owed a *debt* to all people, and he should preach the Good News to them, 1.14. We should also try to pay this debt and tell those around us about God's love.

4/7   11. We should love our neighbours, especially because the Lord will soon return. When we first believed, we were *saved* because God forgave our sins. We have seen that the Holy Spirit wants to save us from the power of sin every day. When the Lord Jesus Christ comes back He will give us new bodies and take us to heaven. Then we will never sin again; we will be saved from the power of sin forever.

No one would want to be asleep when the Lord comes. The apostle does not mean the natural sleep which our bodies need. He is referring to sleep as a picture of laziness. We should be busy serving the Lord; it will make Him happy if He finds us doing His will when He comes, Luke 12.37,43. So the Holy Spirit tells us here to **wake up**, Ephesians 5.14; 1 Thessalonians 5.6.

12. The dark night is a picture of the world while the Lord Jesus is away. When He comes back it will be like a new day, a wonderful day, Malachi 4.2. The Bible tells us what will happen in the last days just before the Lord comes. We can see these things taking place in the world around us today. Paul looked forward to the coming of the Lord; this great day is much closer now than when Paul wrote these words.

The people of this world commit many sins at *night;* some steal, some get drunk, John 3.19; 1 Thessalonians 5.2,7. We did some of these things too before we were saved, but now we should stop doing them, Ephesians 5.11, and be prepared to fight against Satan and all the power of sin, James 4.7. We can put on *armour* to protect ourselves from the enemy, v.14.

13. The devil would like to accuse us if we do anything wrong. Therefore we should be careful to live properly for we cannot hide our acts. The people of the world will know if Christians go to wild parties and get drunk or commit sin. They will know if we fight among ourselves, and will just laugh when we try to tell them about Christ.

14. Still we have enemies: Satan and the world around us, and the old sinful nature, the *flesh.* We should (1) put on the Lord Jesus Christ as our armour, Galatians 3.27, and (2) stop thinking about our own desires.

A soldier wears his armour to protect his body in a fight, and he also has weapons to drive off his enemy. We are told to act like good soldiers of Jesus Christ, 2 Timothy 2.3, and the Holy Spirit tells us about our armour in Ephesians 6.10-17. The Lord Jesus won the victory over Satan by using the Scripture, which is the *sword* of the Spirit. We should put on the Lord Jesus as our armour; He will protect us from all our enemies. He will also help us to control our thoughts. We should not think about evil things, nor make plans which will make it possible for us to commit sin.

The Holy Spirit tells us to give our bodies as a living sacrifice to God, 12.1. In 13.14, He tells us to put on the

Lord Jesus Christ, who will protect us from our enemies. In these two chapters there are many commands which show us how to live in this world; in chapter 14 we will read some more.

4/8   **TEST YOURSELF ON CHAPTER 13**

1. Who gives the government the authority to tell me what I must do?
2. Why should I obey the government? Give two reasons.
3. What should I do if the government makes me pay unfair taxes?
4. Which command contains in short form the other commands? Which other command is even greater than this?
5. Why do we think that the Lord Jesus will soon come back again?
6. What are the three main enemies of every Christian?
7. How can I fight against the flesh?

Check your answers on page 143

A weak brother, 14.1 - 15.7

4/9   The Holy Spirit has told us to love one another, 12.9,10; 13.8-10; to help others in the assembly, 12.4-8; and to live together in peace, 12.18. The local church is like the body of Christ. There are many different parts in a body, but all members try to help the rest. Christ is the head of the body, the Church.

In every church different people have different thoughts about some things. We should try to understand each other, not fight about little differences. Some of the Christians in the assembly at Rome had been Jews until they were saved. The religious leaders of Israel taught that Jews should not eat the meat of animals which had been offered as a sacrifice to heathen idols. They also taught that Jews should keep the seventh day of every week as a sabbath to Jehovah. Many other days were set apart every year for religious purposes. Most of these rules were based on the commands of the Lord in the Old Testament.

We have seen that we can be saved only by believing in the Lord Jesus Christ, not by keeping laws. Some believers are trusting in Christ, but still they feel they must keep some of the laws. Their faith is still *weak,* and they do not understand that we have been set free from law, 6.14; 7.4; 8.2.

In the assembly at Rome, there were those who believed it was wrong to eat some kinds of meat, and it was right to keep certain days as holy days. These believers are called **weak** *brothers, vs.1-5. They do these things because they love the Lord, and they must give account to Him, vs.6-12. We should receive them and be kind to them, vs.13-23.*

Who is a weak brother? 14.1-5

1,2. We should receive and welcome a brother whose faith is weak, but we should not try to argue with him. Some believers in Rome refused to eat any kind of meat, and used only vegetables for their food.

3. The Holy Spirit tells us that we should not judge others on such things. Those who eat any kind of meat are called *strong in the faith,* but they should not think they are better than others. Those who do not eat meat should not think they are holier than those who do. The Lord has accepted every believer. **4.** Every believer is a servant of the Lord, and servants must not judge one another, or think that others will fall into sin. I might say that another believer eats meat which has been offered to idols, and no doubt he will soon do worse things. The Lord has received that believer and He can help him to stand firm.

> The church must judge a believer who is going on in sin, 1 Corinthians 5. But no one needs to go on in sin; the Lord can make him stand.

4/10   **5.** Another brother "weak" in the faith thinks some days every year are more important than others, while the strong Christian knows that every day of his life belongs to the Lord. Each one should try to understand the Lord's will, and not do things just because someone else does them. This verse does not mean that everyone can have his own opinion. All our thoughts must be brought under the control of God's Word.

The weak brother and the Lord, 14.6-12

6. We should be kind to those who sincerely keep certain days, if they are doing it to honour the Lord. Believers who eat ordinary meat give thanks to God for it. Those who eat only vegetables also give thanks to God. We should not judge other believers on such small matters.

> Some of the Jews tried to tell the young Christians that to be saved they must obey the law, and keep certain holy days. The Spirit does not tell us to overlook such false teaching. Paul was afraid the Galatians would go back to law, and he told the Colossian believers not to let anyone put such rules on them, Galatians 4.10,11; Colossians 2.16.

7,8. The apostle has been speaking of eating meat, and keeping holy days, but the whole life of the believer belongs to the Lord. We should not live for ourselves, but for the Lord, and we cannot choose when or how we will die. The life and death of the believer are for the glory of the Lord. **9.** The Lord Jesus died once, and is now alive. He is Lord of all believers, living and dead. Christ is the *Judge* of all men, Acts 10.42, but all do not accept Him as *Lord* today.

> It is very wrong for a Christian to kill himself. He may have to suffer great pain or face terrible problems, but the Lord will surely help him. People who do not know the Lord may become very much afraid when they know they are going to die. But the believer knows that he will go right to the Lord, and this gives him wonderful peace. [Name three men who killed themselves, 1 Samuel 31.4; 2 Samuel 17.23; Matthew 27.5.]

4/11   **10.** The weak Christian should not say the strong one is doing wrong when he eats any kind of meat. And the strong Christian

---

* A little book by D. R. Harris will help you to understand what the Bible teaches about the sabbath day. It is called "Should a Christian Keep the Sabbath day?"

should not look down on the other because his faith is weak. We should not judge another Christian because **God** is the Judge of all men. **11.** The Holy Spirit uses words from Isaiah 45.23 to prove this statement. Every person who has ever lived must bow before the Lord Jesus, even wicked spirits in the world below, Philippians 2.10. We see that the Lord Jesus is God, and that He will judge all creatures, John 5.22.

12. The Lord Jesus will not judge believers as if they were sinners, because we have been justified by His blood, 5.9. But we will all stand before Christ; some will receive rewards for serving Him, 2 Corinthians 5.10, 1 Peter 5.4. Others will be ashamed and lose their rewards, 1 John 2.28; Revelation 3.11, but no one will lose his eternal life, 1 Corinthians 3.15.

> This great truth should make us love God and try to serve Him more.

Strong and weak brothers, 14.13-23

4/12   *We should love our weaker brothers, vs.13-15, and live with them in a peaceful way, vs.16-19. We should do everything in faith, vs.20-23.*

13. The Lord does not want us to judge one another about things like eating meat, or keeping certain holy days. He does want us to help one another. We should never do or say anything which will lead a younger Christian to fall into sin. **14.** The Lord Jesus showed Paul that food itself is not sinful. The Lord taught His disciples that all food is clean, Mark 7.14-23. The weak Christians in Rome should have known this, but those who did know should not have judged those who did not know. It is sinful for a man to go against his own conscience.

> The Holy Spirit here is speaking of things which are not really important. Some Christians try to go on in sin, and say that they are not doing anything wrong. We must try to help them to stop living in sin.

15. A strong brother knows that he can eat any kind of food. But this may hurt weak brothers, and they can get careless about more important things. It would be better for me to stop eating anything which will hurt my brother. The Lord Jesus died for him as well as for me! I must **love** him and act in a loving way toward him.

16. It is good to be strong in faith, and not to be under rules and laws. But I should not use my liberty if it will hurt a weak brother. People would talk about it, and this would not help the work of the Lord. **17.** We are all in the Kingdom of God, which means we are under God's *authority;* He is our Lord. We do not show this by what we eat and drink, but by living as Christ did. He was perfectly righteous and always obeyed His Father. He knew His Father was taking care of Him, and so He always had perfect **peace.** His joy was to do His Father's will, and to bring men back to God, John 4.34; Luke 15.6. We have righteousness, peace and joy, 5.1, 11, and the Holy Spirit will help us to show these things every day. **18.** God will be pleased with those who serve Christ in this way and men will approve if they see we have righteousness, peace and joy in our daily lives.

4/13 **19.** The most important thing is to please God, but we should also try to live in peace with our brothers. We can strengthen each other by building up each other in the faith, 1 Thessalonians 5.11. **20.** I should not insist on eating meat if it will make another brother fall into sin. God has saved him so he can serve the Lord. I might spoil my brother's service for the Lord if I do what he thinks is wrong. It is not a sin to eat any kind of food, but it is a sin to eat anything which I **or** my brother **think** is wrong. **21.** The same is true of anything I do. I should not eat meat or drink wine, or do anything which might make my brother fall into sin, 1 Corinthians 8.13.

22. The strong brother has **faith**, and knows he is not under rules and laws. He should thank the Lord for this but not try to show others that he is wiser or more spiritual than they. He will be happy if he does not have to judge himself for causing a weak brother to fall. **23.** It is wrong for any Christian to act against his conscience. The weak brother may eat meat but he thinks it is wrong to do so. For him it **is** sin, and he feels that he is not pleasing the Lord. This does not mean that he loses his salvation, but he loses his joy in Christ and this is very bad.

The same thing is true of whatever we do. We must live by faith, 1.17. Everything else is sin. Someone may eat meat just to follow the example of an older Christian, but he thinks it is wrong, and so it is. It is wrong to do anything which he *thinks* is wrong.

4/14   **TEST YOURSELF ON CHAPTER 14**
  1. Why does the Bible say some Christians are weak in
     the faith?
  2. Why is it wrong to criticize a servant of the Lord?
  3. What does a strong Christian think about the different
     days of the year?
  4. We should not judge a Christian who thinks he should
     keep the sabbath day, but some people teach that we
     must keep it or we will be lost. What should we do
     about this?
  5. What will happen at the judgment seat of Christ?
  6. Does chapter 14 teach that Christians should let other
     Christians do as they please?

Check your answers on page 143

Help one another, 15.1-6

4/15   *The Holy Spirit teaches us more about this subject in 15.1-6.*
We should help each other, vs.1,2; and follow the example of the
Lord Jesus Christ, vs.3,4. The apostle prayed that God would help
the Roman Christians in these things, vs.5,6.

1. We have been told in chapter 14 that we should not cause
a weak brother to fall into sin. Instead those who are strong in faith
should be willing to help others who are weak, Galatians 6.2. Most
people live only to please themselves. 2. We should try to please
our brothers; this means to help them spiritually, so they will have
greater joy as Christians. 3. Even the Lord Jesus Christ did not try
to please Himself. He wanted to help men, Mark 10.45, and to
please His Father. Men hated God, and so they hated and insulted
God's Son, John 15.24. The Holy Spirit used the words of Psalm
69.9 which the Lord Jesus could have said about Himself. David
wrote the 69th Psalm and told about his great troubles, but the

Holy Spirit led him on to use words which the Messiah could use.

Christ suffered because men spoke against Him and killed Him. Surely we can give up our own pleasure if it will help another believer.

In the New Testament, the Holy Spirit quoted many Old Testament verses, and these help us to understand both the Old Testament and the New Testament. In verse 4, He tells us that **all** of the Old Testament was written to teach us important lessons. The whole Bible helps us to have *patience* when we are in trouble, and it *encourages* us when we are sad. It also gives us a strong *hope* because we know that the Lord Jesus is coming back again.

Some Christians love the New Testament, but think they do not need to read the Old Testament. Others just read a small part of the Old Testament. But the whole Bible is from God. The Old Testament teaches us a great deal of wonderful truth about God.

5. Paul prayed that God would help the Christians at Rome to agree with one another, and live in peace. The Scriptures give us patience, and encourage us, but these things really come from God **through** His Book. We can live together in peace if we grow more and more like the Lord Jesus. **6.** The most important thing we can do is to worship and praise God. The Father is seeking for those who will worship Him in spirit and in truth, John 4.23. Christians should love one another, and agree to praise God together, the God and Father of our Lord Jesus Christ.

The Lord Jesus is in heaven at God's right hand, and He is always praying for His people. Before He went back to heaven, He gave us an example of how He would pray for us, John 17. The Holy Spirit led Paul to pray for the believers in Rome and in other cities. We can be sure the Lord Jesus is praying for us today in the same way, because this is God's will for us.

Our relation to all men, 15.7-33

4/16 *We should receive all believers, v.7, and give the Good News to all other people. Christ taught God's truth to the Jews, so they would teach men of other nations, vs.8-13. The Lord commanded Paul to preach the Good News to the Gentiles, vs.14-33.*

Receive all true believers, 15.7

The Lord Jesus Christ invites all men to come to Him, Matthew 11.28. This is for the glory of God; so was everything which the Lord did. We love the Lord and should do as He does: we should receive all true believers, for *God's* glory. We should receive them into the church and into our homes, 3 John 8, but only if this will bring glory to God.

The Jews should have taught men about God, 15.8-13

8. Many believers in Rome had been born Jews, and some of them were *weak in faith;* they thought they should obey many rules about eating meat or keeping holy days. The Lord Jesus came to serve the nation of Israel, Matthew 15.24. God had promised the early ancestors of Israel that He would give great blessing to their descendants. These promises were true and Christ came to bless Israel. Gentile Christians should love all Jewish brothers.

4/17   **9-12.** God also wanted to show His great mercy to the Gentiles so they too would praise Him. Jewish Christians should love their Gentile brothers. The Holy Spirit used four verses from the Old Testament to prove that God had always wanted people of Gentile nations to praise Him.

1. David thanked God for saving him from all his enemies, and promised to praise the Lord when he was with Gentile people also, Psalm 18.49.

2. Before that, Moses praised the Lord for blessing His people and called on Gentile nations to rejoice with them, Deuteronomy 32.43.

3. Psalm 117 is the shortest psalm, shorter than any chapter in the Bible. In it a servant of God invited all nations to thank the Lord because He is kind to His people, and His truth will continue forever.

4. Isaiah announced that Messiah would come to rule over the Gentiles, and they would put their hopes in Him, Isaiah 11.10. The Holy Spirit led Isaiah and Paul to call Christ *the root of Jesse,* who was the father of David, Matthew 1.6. As a Man the Lord Jesus was the *descendant* of David and of Jesse, and is called the *branch* of Jesse in Isaiah 11.1. But the root of the tree is not the same as a branch. God is the *root* of the whole

family of men, and Adam is called God's son, Luke 3.38. The
Lord Jesus, God the Son, is the Creator of all men, John 1.3.

   The Lord taught the Jews the same truth when He asked
them about Himself. They said the Christ was David's son,
but David called him *Lord,* Psalm 110.1; Mark 12.35-37.
Both are true: the Messiah is the Son of David, and the
Lord of David. In the same way He is both Root and Branch
of Jesse: the Creator of Jesse (and of all men) and the Descendant of Jesse. We can safely put our hopes in Him, and
trust Him to rule us wisely.

   13. Then we have another prayer of Paul as led by the Holy
Spirit. God gives us hope, and He will fill us with great joy and
peace if we believe fully in Him. The Holy Spirit is able to give us
the hope which will keep on growing until the Lord Himself comes
back for us.

The Lord commanded Paul to preach to the Gentiles, 15.14-33

4/18   Paul explained how he obeyed the Lord's command, vs.14-21.
He planned to visit the Christians in Rome, vs.22-29, and asked
them to pray for him, vs.30-33.

Paul's methods, 15.14-21

   *Paul preached the Good News to many Gentiles, but he knew
that he could only reach a few of the millions of people who
needed to hear. Therefore he was also careful to teach the Christians
so they could go out and reach others with the message of Christ.
Here he tells us first about the assembly, vs.14-16; then about his
work in the gospel, vs.17-21.*

   14. Paul wrote this whole letter to the believers at Rome, but
he knew that they were Christians and had already learned a good
deal about God. They were able to teach and advise each other
how to know and do God's will. We see from the New Testament
that the early Christians could teach and encourage each other
when they met together, 1 Corinthians 14.26.

   15,16. Still Paul had written boldly about things which they
needed to remember. God had given Paul his authority, but Paul
knew that it was only through God's grace. God appointed Paul to
serve Christ Jesus as a priest by preaching the Good News to the
Gentiles. As a priest he had the privilege of making an offering to

God, Hebrews 5.1. The Lord had blessed Paul's service, and given him *fruit:* many Gentile Christians. Paul presented them as an offering to God. Every sacrifice had to be perfect, and the Holy Spirit Himself knew these believers in advance and had set them aside for God.

4/19 **17.** This made Paul very happy, but he knew that he could serve God only by living in union with Christ. So he tells us a little about his work preaching the gospel.

18. Paul did not want anyone to think that he was proud of his work for the Lord. He spoke here only about what Christ had done through him. Paul had preached the Good News, and this message brought many Gentiles to obey God. They listened to his words and they saw what he did, and all that he suffered for the Lord. **19.** Paul sometimes performed signs and miracles, Acts 13.11; 14.10; 19.11; 28.8, and these wonders persuaded some of the people that God was with him. Above all, only the power of the Holy Spirit could really lead people to believe in Christ, 1 Corinthians 2.4. Paul knew God was with him, and he wanted all men to hear the Good News of our Lord Jesus Christ. He preached in Jerusalem, Acts 9.26-29; 15.2,12; 22.1-21; he also preached in many other cities and countries. We can read about his experiences in Macedonia, which was far to the north, Acts 16.9 - 17.14. If you have maps in the back of your Bible you will see that Illyricum is still further north. Wherever he went, Paul preached the Good News *fully.* He preached to all who would listen and he told them the whole truth of God, Acts 20.27.

20. Paul's desire was to preach the Good News in places where people had never heard about Christ, not to add to a work which someone else had started. At first it is hard to preach the Good News in any place, and later it is often a little easier. Paul wanted to obey the command of the Lord Jesus when He said we should preach the Gospel to all men, Mark 16.15. **21.** Isaiah had prophesied that the Gentile nations would see and understand things which they had never known before, Isaiah 52.15.

The apostle Paul also had a great desire to please the Lord, 2 Corinthians 5.9. Of course you cannot please Him unless you obey Him. Are there places today where people do not know the name of Christ? There are millions of

people like that. Perhaps there are Christians and a few
churches in your city, but many people do not know the
Good News. Every child must be told about the Lord Jesus.
You can please the Lord by telling them about Him.

Paul's plans, 15.22-29

4/20 *We have seen that Paul wanted to build up the churches, vs. 14-*
16, and to preach the Good News, vs.18-20. Here we read about
his plan to go to Rome to help the believers there, vs.22,23; then
to Spain to preach the Good News where Christ had not been
named, v.24. First he had to go to Jerusalem, vs.25-27; then he
wanted to go on toward the west, with the Lord's blessing, vs.28,29.

22. Paul had given years of his life to preach where Christ
had not been named, and so he had not been able to visit the
Christians in Rome. Christ had been named in Rome, there was
already an assembly there, but Paul wanted to visit them to teach
them more about the Lord, 1.10-13. **23.** Now he began to hope that
he could go to Rome. Paul was in the city of Corinth in Greece
when he wrote this letter. He had been in Corinth for one and a
half years, and three months more in Greece, Acts 18.11; 20.3.
The Holy Spirit showed him that his work there was finished so
that he could think about going to Rome.

24. Spain was much further west of Rome than Rome was
from Corinth. Spain must have seemed like the end of the earth
to the disciples when the Lord told them to witness to Him **every-**
where, Acts 1.8. Paul thought he could visit the believers in Rome
for a short time on his way to Spain. He would enjoy such a visit,
and the Christians might want to help him on his way, 3 John 6.

4/21 **25,26.** First of all he was going to Jerusalem. Many of the
saints in Jerusalem were poor, and the Christians in Macedonia and
Greece (or Achaia) wanted to send some money to help them,
Acts 19.21; 20.22; 2 Corinthians 8.1-5; 9.1-5. **27.** God gave the
Good News first to the Jews, 3.2; 9.5; 15.8, and these Gentiles re-
ceived many blessings through the Jews. So it was right that the
Gentiles should share their money with the Jews when they needed
help.

28. Paul felt that he was responsible to take this money to
Jerusalem, and to see that it was given to the right persons. After

that he would be able to go to Rome, and then on to Spain. **29.** He knew that he would bring the believers at Rome a blessing from the Lord. He would teach them more of God's holy Word, especially about Christ, and this would help them very much.

Paul asked the Christians to pray for him, 15.30-33

4/22   *He asked them to pray for three things, vs.30-32, and then he prayed for them, v.33.*

30. Paul encouraged the believers to join with him in praying for these three things. He asked for this because Jesus Christ was their Lord, and because the Holy Spirit had given them real love for Paul.

> Some Christians think it is easy to pray, but Paul knew that there were many spiritual enemies who would like to ruin his work for the Lord, Ephesians 6.12. So he told the believers to pray *fervently*, as Epaphras did, Colossians 4.12. We should learn to pray in this way.

31. Paul knew that many Jews at Jerusalem hated him because he preached about Christ to the Gentiles. They tried to kill him the first time he went back to Jerusalem after he had turned to the Lord, Acts 9.29. So he asked the Christians to pray that he might be kept safe again this time. Even some of the believers in Jerusalem had been afraid of Paul at first, Acts 9.26, and later some did not like the way he taught the Gentile Christians, Acts 15.5. Paul hoped that they would not be too proud to accept the money which he was bringing from the Gentile Christians. **32.** Then he asked the Christians to pray that he might come to them in Rome, and enjoy his visit with them.

> Did God answer these prayers? We know that God always answers our prayers, John 14.13, but not always in the way or at the time we expected.

The Christians at Jerusalem did indeed accept Paul, and the gift he brought. The Jews tried to kill him, but the Lord kept him safe, Acts 21.17,31; 23.12, 31-33. However, he was in prison in Jerusalem and in Caesarea for two years, Acts 24.27. God answered prayer, but Paul had to suffer for the Lord Jesus' sake. Finally he got to Rome, but he was still a prisoner. He had some freedom and could talk to his friends and preach about the kingdom of God,

Acts 28.16,30,31. He also wrote four letters while in Rome: Colossians, Philemon, Ephesians, and Philippians.

The Bible teaches us a great deal about prayer, and we should learn how to pray. But we must remember to ask only for God's will, as Paul did, and then thank the Lord for His answer.

33. Then Paul by the Holy Spirit asked that God would be with them. He called God, the *God of Peace,* who would give them peace in their hearts while they prayed that Paul might be kept safe on his dangerous journey. Paul prayed for the Christians according to God's will, as the Holy Spirit led him. The Lord Jesus is praying for us, also according to the will of God. Think of Paul's prayers as examples of how Christ is praying for us today, 15.5, 13,33; 16.20.

4/23 **TEST YOURSELF ON CHAPTER 15**

1. Did the Lord Jesus Christ try to please men?
2. Does the Bible say we should receive *all* believers?
3. Why did Christ come into this world, verses 8 and 9?
4. Where does the Old Testament teach that God wants the Gentiles to hear about His love?
5. Why does the Bible call Christ both the root and branch of Jesse?
6. What kind of *fruit* did God give to Paul?
7. Will miracles persuade men to accept Christ?
8. Why had Paul never visited Rome before?
9. What three things did Paul ask the Christians to pray for?
10. Were these prayers answered?

Check your answers on page 144

GOD HONOURS
HIS PEOPLE
WHO SERVE HIM
chapter 16

*4/24   We now come to the last section and the last chapter of the letter to the Romans. Here Paul mentioned the names of many Christians, some in Rome, some in Corinth. First he asked the Christians in Rome to receive a sister in Christ, vs.1,2. Then he sent greetings to some of the people in Rome and said something good about most of them, vs.3-16. He told them **not** to receive people who would just cause trouble, vs.17-20. Other believers who were with Paul also sent their greetings to the Christians in Rome, vs.21-24. Then Paul ended his letter by giving praise to the only wise God, vs.25-27.*

Paul recommended Phoebe, 16.1,2

Phoebe was a wealthy woman, a sister in Christ, who was a great help in the assembly at Cenchrea, a small town near Corinth. She was going to Rome, and Paul may have asked her to carry this letter to the believers there. So he asked them to receive her as a Christian and help her if she needed anything. Paul told them that she had often helped him, and many others also.

Paul's friends in Rome, 16.3-16

4/25   Paul had never been to Rome, but he had many friends there. He mentioned 26 people in these verses, about eight of them women, but we do not know much about any of them.

3,4. Aquilla and his wife Priscilla, however, had been with Paul before, in Corinth, Acts 18.1-3. Paul as a boy had learned to make tents and he often earned money that way. Aquilla and Priscilla were also tent-makers, so Paul lived with them. The Emperor Claudius had made all Jews and Jewish Christians leave Rome, so Aquilla and Priscilla went to Corinth. However, they were allowed to return and were in Rome when Paul wrote this letter. Paul had taught them a good deal of truth and they were able to teach Apollos many things which he did not know, Acts 18.24-26. In Rome the church held meetings in the home of Aquilla and Priscilla. The assembly in Ephesus also met in their home, because Paul was in Ephesus when he wrote 1 Corinthians 16.19. Here Paul said they worked with him in the Lord's service and even risked their lives for him. He thanked God for Aquilla and Priscilla and so did many others.

5. Paul sent his greetings to the little assembly which met in their home. Paul loved Epaenetus, especially because he was the first person in the province of Asia whom Paul led to Christ.

6,7. There are several women named Mary in the New Testament. This one had helped Paul and his companions before she went to Rome. Andronicus and Junias were Jews who had been saved before Paul was. They had also suffered with him in prison, and were well known to the apostles.

4/26 **8-11.** Paul loved Ampliatus, and Stachys; Urbanus had helped him in the Lord's work. Apelles had gone through some time of testing, and had stood firm for Christ. Paul sent his greetings to Aristobulus, and Narcissus, and their families and workmen; to Herodion, another Jewish Christian.

4/27 **12-15.** Tryphaena, and Tryphosa, and Persis had served the Lord. Rufus may be a man from Cyrene, who was mentioned in Mark 15.21. Paul spoke about Rufus' mother as if she were his own, perhaps because she had helped Paul as a mother would. Paul sent his greetings also to other groups of Christians, who probably met in different houses in Rome.

16. Paul told the believers to love one another, 13.8-10; 12.9, 10; 14.15; and now he told them to greet one another in a loving way, with a holy kiss, 1 Corinthians 16.20; 2 Corinthians 13.12; 1 Thessalonians 5.26; 1 Peter 5.14. In the Roman world, men often greeted other men with a kiss, and women greeted women in the same way. Paul said it should be a *holy* kiss. The Holy Spirit will never lead us into temptation, Matthew 6.13, because God wants us to be holy, as He is, 1 Peter 1.15.

Other churches also sent their greetings as well as Paul.

Do not receive trouble makers, 16.17-20

4/28   **17.** We have been told to receive true believers, even those who are still weak in the faith, 14.1; 15.7. But some people were causing trouble by teaching doctrine which was different from what the apostles taught. This was upsetting the faith of some of the Christians, and Paul told them to keep away from such people.

> We should not allow false teachers to stay in the church. We should warn them twice, then ask them to leave, Titus 3.10. We must never receive those who deny the doctrine of Christ, 2 John 9,10. This means that every believer must understand what God's Word teaches, so he will know what to do.

18. These people try to act as if they were serving Christ, but the Holy Spirit tells us here they are really doing everything just to please themselves. They are slaves to their own appetites - they live only for the flesh, Philippians 3.19. They are good talkers, and will tell you that you are a wonderful person. Simple people believe them, and think they are teaching the truth.

19. Paul knew that the Christians in Rome were not *simple,* but had already learned God's will. Everyone had heard that they obeyed the Lord and this made Paul happy. Still he wrote very plainly to them, because the Holy Spirit wanted them to be wise about what is good, and not learn what is wrong.

> Satan told Eve that she and Adam would know good and evil if they did what was evil. God wants us to know what is good, and do it. It is never God's will for us to commit sin.

20. Then the Holy Spirit promised them that God would soon crush Satan under their feet. God will show all creatures that Christ has defeated Satan, and that Christians share in His victory, Revelation 20.10. God had promised that a *man* would overcome Satan, Genesis 3.15; this was the Man Christ Jesus. Jehovah promised Christ that He would put His feet on His enemies, Psalm 110.1. Joshua told the officers of his army to put their feet on the necks of their enemies, Joshua 10.24.

Paul's letters start with *grace* and *peace,* Romans 1.7. Every letter of Paul ends with the prayer that the *grace* of the Lord Jesus Christ should be with those who read it.

Several people in Corinth sent their greetings to the believers in Rome, 16.21-24

4/29 **21.** Timothy worked with Paul for many years, Acts 16.3; 17.14; 18.5; 19.22; 20.4; 1 Corinthians 4.17; 16.10; Philippians 2.19; 1 Thessalonians 3.2,6. He was with Paul when he wrote to some of the churches, 2 Corinthians 1.1; Philippians 1.1; Colossians 1.1; 1 Thessalonians 1.1; 2 Thessalonians 1.1; Philemon 1. Paul wrote two letters to Timothy, and he asked him to come to him when he was in prison near the end of his life, 2 Timothy 4.9.

The other three men were Jews, and we can learn a little about them in Acts 13.1; 17.5; and 20.4. [Where did Lucius live? _____ Where did Jason live? _____]

22. Paul usually asked someone to write his letters for him, and Tertius wrote to the Romans. He, too, sent his greetings in the Lord, v.**23.** So did Gaius, Erastus, and Quartus. Paul had baptized Gaius, 1 Corinthians 1.14, and was living in his home when he wrote this letter. Erastus was a very important officer in the city of Corinth, but Paul could say nothing about Quartus, except that he was a brother in the Lord.

Chapter 16 makes us think of the judgment seat of Christ. Only true Christians will be there, and the Lord Jesus will know us all by name. He will say something good about each one if He can. He will call some *good and faithful servants,* and this will bring them great pleasure. Of course, He will say it only if it is true. He will not call us good and faithful if we have been poor servants or unfaithful.

Some people will be received into heaven, but the Lord Jesus cannot say anything good about them. They are born again, they are *brothers* in the family of God, but have never served God in any way. They are like Quartus, a *brother.*

24. Most old Bibles do not have verse 24, but Paul has already written this prayer that the Lord's grace should be with us, v.20.

Praise to God, 16.25-27

4/30 *The last three verses also make us think of heaven, because there we will praise God forever. God has all power, v.25; He is eternal, v.26, and knows everything, v.27.*

25. Paul said that the Good News is God's power to save all men, 1.16. Now he adds that God has power to make us stand strong in the faith. The Lord is able to make us *stand*, 14.4. The Good News tells us that we should do this, but we can do it only with God's help. Paul preached about Jesus Christ so that men can be saved, **and** learn to do God's will. God's great plan has always been that the Gentiles should be blessed through the Gospel, but He did not fully reveal it in earlier ages.

26. Now God has revealed His wonderful plan. The Holy Spirit had just guided Paul to write this letter, and other parts of the New Testament were written before this. These are some of the *writings of the prophets,* which make plain God's plan in the Gospel. The rest of the New Testament was written later, and it all agrees with this.

The Eternal God has no beginning or end. He created everything else in the world, and He has complete authority over all His creatures. He has commanded us to tell all nations about His love: He wants them to believe and obey, 1.5.

These verses give us in short form, the main teaching of Romans. We are justified when we believe; we show this by obeying. We should pass on this teaching to others.

27. What a wonderful plan! Paul gave glory to the only wise God who will be glorified through Jesus Christ forever. We can all say **Amen**, to show that we want it to be so, 1.25; 9.5; 11.36; 15.33.

TEST YOURSELF ON CHAPTER 16

1. Why did Paul ask the Christians at Rome to help Phebe?
2. Why did Paul love Epaenetus?
3. Was Rufus Paul's brother?
4. How can we know when a false teacher comes?
5. What did Paul ask God to give to those who read his letters?
6. How does chapter 16 make us think of heaven?
7. What is the command of the Eternal God?

Check your answers on page 144.

LEARN SOME MORE

ABOUT THE BOOK OF ROMANS

Take a piece of paper about as big as this whole page and cover up everything on this page except what you are reading just now. You can move the paper down a little at a time so you can read more. Each paragraph or section of the page has a line under it. A paragraph with a line under it is called a **frame.** *You should read only one frame at a time, and keep the rest of the page covered with the piece of paper. Each frame will tell you a little more about the book of Romans.*

Each frame also has a question or a space at the end. This is to see if you have understood the main teaching of the frame. Try to answer the question or write the missing word in the empty space. If you cannot answer the question, read the frame again. When you think you know the right answer, move the paper down so you can see the next frame. Before you read anything in the next frame, look first at the **right** *side of the frame. This gives the correct answer to the question in the first frame. If you had the right answer, this shows that you have understood the most important part of the first frame. You are now ready to go on to read everything in the* **second** *frame. IF you did not get the right answer, you are not ready to go on. You should read the first frame again and really try to understand it. When you understand the first frame then you can go on to the second frame. Read this frame carefully and answer the question at the end. Then go on to the third frame and all the others, one by one.*

1. You have now read through Paul's letter to the Romans, also this book which explains it. Every book in the Bible tells something about God and Christ and Man. We will now ask, What does Romans teach about these great subjects? But first let us see what the Holy Spirit teaches about the Bible itself. We know that the 66 books of the Bible are the Word of God. They tell us the truth of God. Paul said that God's prophets spoke in the Holy Scriptures, 1.2. They were *God's* prophets, so we know they spoke the truth. The Scriptures are called *Holy,* but the Spirit never called any books *Holy* if they contained what is false. What two words in 1.2 **prove that the Bible is true?** ....

2. God's prophets wrote the Holy Scriptures as the Spirit   *1. His (God's)*
led them, 2 Peter 1.21. The same Holy Spirit quoted from   *Holy*
the Old Testament books about 70 times in the letter to the
Romans. Fourteen times Paul said *as it is written* and then used words from
the Old Testament, for example, 1.17. So we see that the Spirit honoured
the Old Testament Scriptures when He .... from them.

----

3. The Old Testament Scriptures were written to teach   *2. quoted*
us more about God, 15.4. We should not read or study any
books which are not true. The Scriptures teach us to be patient and they
encourage us to hope in God alone. What three good things can we get if we
learn from the Scriptures? .... , ... , ...

----

4. Many books are helpful, but others try to turn us   *3. Hope*
away from God. We read about *the truth* of God in 3.7, but   *Patience*
men have turned from God's truth and exchanged it for a *Encouragement*
lie, 1.25. We should not read books which turn us away
from the Lord. When men reject the truth of God, what do they have?...........

----

5. Paul by the Holy Spirit taught the Christians at Rome   *4. A lie*
that the Bible is inspired by God. What did Paul teach
in this letter about God Himself? One thing we can learn from the world of
nature is God's *eternal power,* 1.20. God must have had the power to create
the world before time began. God had no beginning and will have no end.
What does 16.26 teach about God? ....

----

6. God is eternal and His power is eternal, 1.20. He used   *5. He is*
His great power to create the world and to save all who   *eternal*
believe, 1.16. His command brings into being what did not
exist before He spoke. This same power can give life to those who are dead,
4.17. God can make us succeed as Christians, 14.4, and in the future His
power will be able to bring the Jews back to Himself, 11.23. We see that
Romans teaches about God's power in creation and in ....

----

7. God's power is great enough to make Him supreme   *6. Salvation or*
over all His creatures. There is only one true God, 3.30,   *Redemption*
although men worship other creatures, 1.23,25. God has
power on earth and He can control the governments of all countries, 13.1.
From these verses and many others we can be sure that there is ....
God and He is ....,. over all creatures.

----

8. We also learn that God knows everything. He even knows the secrets which men keep in their minds and God will some day judge all sinful thoughts, 2.16. We read about God's wisdom and knowledge in 11.33. Who only is *all wise?* See 16.27.
....

7. one supreme

---

9. Man can never find out by his own wisdom what God is like, but God in His grace has revealed Himself. God revealed His power when He created the earth, 1.20. He has revealed His righteousness and His grace in the Scriptures, and many verses in Romans teach us these things. The righteousness of God is mentioned seven times in Romans, for example, 1.17; 3.21. God is fair when He judges men, 1.24,26, 28, and will not give special favours to anyone, 2.11. The judgment of God, 1.32; 2.3, is righteous judgment, 2.5. The Old Testament reveals God's righteousness very fully, but the Jews did not really understand it, 10.3. Now in the New Testament God has revealed that He can righteously accept all those who believe in Christ, 3.22. The Good News reveals both God's grace and His ....

8. God

---

10. In Romans we read about the grace of God, 5.15; His mercy, 9.16; 12.1; His kindness, 2.4; and His gift, 6.23. God calls us His beloved, 1.7, and has shown us how much He loves us, 5.8. Nothing can separate us from the love of Christ or the love of God, 8.35,39; and His love is poured into our hearts, 5.5. God is our Father, 1.7; 6.4; 8.15. How has God proved that He loves us? ....
....

9. Righteousness

---

11. The Holy Spirit in Romans has taught us many things about God and many more about **Christ.** Christ is called the Son of God seven times: 1.3,4,9; 5.10; 8.3, 29,32; God is called His Father, 15.6. We have seen that Christ is called **God** who rules over all, and should be praised for ever, 9.5. The Good News is about our Lord Jesus Christ and the first thing we should know about Him is that He is ....

10. Christ died for us while we were yet sinners, 5.8.

---

12. God sent His Son into this world to do what His Father wanted, 8.3. The Son became a Man, a Descendant of David, 1.3. He is called Man, 5.15, and other books in the Bible show us that He was a complete Man with body, soul and spirit. He lived a perfect life in this world and always pleased His Father, 15.3. The Son of God became .... and lived a .... life in this world.

11. The Son of God

---

13. Why did the only perfect Man have to die? God   *12. Man*
planned it and chose the time when Christ would die, 5.6.   *perfect*
We were sinners at that time, 5.8, but through Christ's death
God can forgive us, 3.25. More still, we are made right with God, 5.9, no one
can condemn us, 8.34. Christ died so that He could become the Lord of all
men, 14.9. We can say Christ died so God can forgive all our sins and make
Him the .... of all.

_____

14. God raised Christ from death, 4.24; 8.11; 10.9, and   *13. Lord*
the Lord will never die again, 6.9. The Father had the
power to raise Christ, 6.4, and He is now at God's right hand, 8.34. God raised
Christ to prove that He is the Son of God and to justify all who believe in
Him, 4.25. God raised Christ from death and put Him in a place of great
..................; this proves that Christ is ....

_____

15. Many Christians look back to the time when   *14. honour or glory*
Christ died and they put their trust in Him. We should   *the Son of God*
also thank the Lord for His *present* work for us. Christ
was raised to life and now He prays to God for us so that no one can condemn
us, 8.34. We are saved every day from the power of sin because Christ is alive,
5.10, and so we can live a new life, 6.4. Christ is alive in heaven and He helps
us to live the .... life in this world.

_____

16. The Lord Jesus will not stay in heaven for ever; He is   *15. new*
coming back again. Paul did not say much about this in Romans,
but we do read that the Lord will judge all men, believers and unbelievers,
14.10; 2.16. Believers will never be condemned, 8.1, but God will punish those
who are wicked, 2.5,8. The Lord Jesus will come back again and ....
.... all men.

_____

17. So we see that the Holy Spirit in Romans taught a   *16. righteously*
great deal about the Lord Jesus Christ. The word Christ is   *judge*
found 68 times in Romans, sometimes with the name Jesus
and sometimes with Lord Jesus. *Jesus* is the name of our Lord when He was a
Man here on earth and Paul used this name by itself only twice in Romans:
3.26 and 8.11. The word *Lord* is used for Jehovah in the Old Testament and
here in Romans it is found 45 times; sometimes it refers to God, sometimes to
the Lord Jesus. So we see that the Lord Jesus is God. Paul wrote about
Christ in glory, so almost always he called Him ....

_____

18. We can learn something about the Holy Spirit   *17. Jesus Christ or*
in Romans. The Spirit is *life* and He is the Spirit of   *Lord Jesus Christ*

God, 8.10,11. He has *power* and gave Paul power to do miracles, 15.13,19. This does not mean that everyone who has the Spirit can do some wonderful things. For example, John the Baptist was filled with the Holy Spirit, but he did not perform any miracles, Luke 1.15; John 10.41. The Holy Spirit is the Spirit of ....

———————————————————————————————————————

19. God gives us His Spirit and the Spirit lives in us, 5.5;   *18. God* 8.9,11,23. What does God the Spirit do for us? He brings us life, 8.2; peace, 8.6; joy, 14.17, and love, 15.30. He controls our minds, 8.5; rules our conscience, 9.1; helps us, 8.13,26; and leads us, 8.14. He shows us we are sons of God and prays for us, 8.15,16,26,27. We can see that the Holy Spirit helps us to live the .... life.

———————————————————————————————————————

20. The Holy Spirit is mentioned 19 times in chapter 8   *19. Christian* alone and in other chapters also. The Holy Spirit is God and was never created, but there are other spirits who were created. Some of these are called angels, but we read about them in Romans only in 8.38: they cannot separate us from the love of God. Of course, only wicked angels would try to take us away from the Lord. Satan himself is mentioned only once in Romans, in 16.20: God will soon crush him. Paul spoke in Romans only of .... angels and taught that they could never .... from God.

———————————————————————————————————————

21. God created spirits and men. Some people try to prove   *20. take us* that men slowly developed from animals, but Paul taught that   *away* Adam was the head of the whole human family. Adam sinned and all men must die, 5.12,14,15,17. We see that Adam's sin affected all his ....

———————————————————————————————————————

22. There is a great difference between men and animals. *21. descendants* Both men and animals have bodies and souls, but only men have **spirits.** You can see and feel the body of a man or of an animal, but you cannot see the soul or the spirit. There is a difference between soul and spirit. In the old Greek Testament we read about the soul in 2.9 and 13.1; and about man's spirit in 8.16 and 12.11. God's Word speaks about our bodies, souls and spirits in 1 Thessalonians 5.23. Men are different from animals because men have ....

———————————————————————————————————————

23. The apostle Paul said a great deal about **sin** in Romans: *22. spirits* he used this word over fifty times. Paul taught that all men have sinned, 3.23 and 5.12, and that God is angry with sin, 1.18. But Christ died for us, for sinners, 5.8; and God can forgive us, 4.7. All men are sinners

and God is angry with sin, but He can .... us because Christ ....
for us.

_____

24. The Lord Jesus died **for** our sins, 4.25: He died **for** wicked   *23. forgive*
people. This was when we were helpless sinners, 5.6,8. Also read   *died*
3.25. The little word .... is important if we want to understand
why Christ died.

_____

25. Christ died for all and all who **believe** will be saved. In Romans   *24. for*
the Holy Spirit says a great deal about believing and having faith, in
fact these words are found 60 times in this letter. How can I get faith? It
comes from hearing, 10.17: so I am glad someone told me. What happened
when I believed? I was saved through faith, 1.16 and 10.9; I am justified
through faith, 3.22,28,30; 9.30; as Abraham was, 4.3. So I get peace and joy,
5.1; 15.13, and life, 1.17. Through faith I get salvation, justification and
....

_____

26. We are saved by faith, so salvation is based on the grace of   *25. peace*
God, 3.24; 4.16; and this is the end of the law, 10.4. We are saved   *joy*
by faith alone, but this does not mean we can disobey God, 1.5;   *life*
16.26. Our faith may be very weak but it will grow stronger.
Abraham's faith was strong, 4.19,20, but some believers still have weak faith,
14.1. We are saved by ...., not works, and this should grow stronger.

_____

27. When we believed in Christ, God forgave our sins and this   *26. faith*
made us very happy, 4.7. But God also **justified** us and this is
more wonderful still. Abraham was justified, 4.3,9; and any man will be
justified if he believes, 4.5,11,23,24. If a man could keep God's law perfectly,
God would declare that he is righteous, 2.13, and he would have something
to boast about, 4.2, but no one has ever done so, 3.20. We are sinners and
God counts us righteous because of His **grace**, 3.24; because **Christ died** for us,
5.9; and because we **believe**, 3.28; 10.10. As a result we have peace with God,
5.1. No man can be justified because of his own works; anyone can be justified
because of God's .... and Christ's ....

_____

28. God can save us from sin. In past time I believed on Christ   *27. grace*
and I was **saved**, 10.9,13. Still I had many old habits and I need   *death*
God's power to help me stop committing sin. This power comes
to me from the living Christ, 5.10, IF I confess with my lips that He is Lord,
10.9,10. When Christ comes we will be saved completely, 5.9; 13.11. So we
can say that our salvation takes place in the past, in the .... and
in the ....

_____

29. God wants to set us free from sin. He does this through our **28. present**
Lord Jesus Christ, 3.24. But we will not be entirely free from sin   **future**
until the Lord comes back, 8.23. We will all be delivered from
the power of sin when Christ ....

---

30. We have eternal life, 5.21; 6.23, and we are now sons of   **29. returns**
God. We are led by God's Spirit, and the Spirit assures us we
are God's sons, 8.14,16. People do not believe that we are the sons of God,
but God will show that we are His sons when Christ comes, 8.17,19,21. We
do not look like .... now, but some day everyone will know that
we have eternal life.

---

31. All true believers have the life of God in them. We   **30. God's sons**
are together like a person's body because the body is made
of many different parts which all have the same life in them. The Bible says
the true Church is like a body, 12.4,5; 1 Corinthians 10.17; Ephesians 4.4.
The Church is like a body because every believer has the .... of God
in him.

---

32. Each part of a man's body helps all the rest of the body, his **31. life**
hand, his foot, his eye and all the rest. So in the **Church**, the body
of Christ, everyone is able to help the others. God has given to every believer
some gifts so he can do something for others. Some can preach or teach, some
can serve or help, some can give or show kindness, 12.6-8. In the body of
Christ every .... is able to .... the rest of the body.

---

33. The prophet Isaiah said that the Saviour would come and   **32. part**
deliver the people of Israel from their sins. We know that the   **help**
Lord Jesus came, but most of the Jews did not receive Him as
their Saviour. Paul used the words of Isaiah to teach that Christ will **come
again** in the future, 11.26. The Holy Spirit wants us to know that ....
.... is coming back again.

---

34. The first time Christ came, men put Him to shame. The **33. The Lord**
second time He will come with great **glory**. We hope to share   **Jesus**
in Christ's glory, 5.2, when it is revealed to us, 8.18. In fact,
God is preparing us for this glory, 9.23. When Christ comes we will be able to
share His .... with Him.

---

35. We now have a **eternal** life, life which will never end, 6.22.   **34. glory**
God is eternal, 16.26, and we will praise Him for ever, 1.25; 9.5;
11.36; 16.27. God has given us .... which will continue for ever.

---

36. God wants to bless all men, but He is angry with those who   *35. life*
refuse to believe on His Son. When Christ comes back, all wicked
persons will be judged, 2.5,8. We have been saved from God's wrath, 5.9; and
we should tell people that they too can be saved. God loves all men, but He
will .... those who reject His Son.

_____

We have heard and believed the Good News.   *36. judge*

We should tell others also.

HERE ARE THE ANSWERS

CHAPTER 1

1. The first, it has only 17 verses.
2. The Good News, see page 9.
3. The Bible uses the word *saints* for all Christians, page 9.
4. God was his Witness, v.9.
5. Because it is God's power to save all who believe, v.16.
6. Men of faith, who believe in the Lord Jesus Christ.
7. Through the world of nature, vs.19, 20.
8. He gives them up, vs.24, 26, 28.
9. They live immoral lives, v.24.
10. No, the Bible teaches that men have turned away from God, vs.18-28.
11. Yes, men who have turned against God do these things, vs.21, 30.
12. No, but these verses show us that we are sinners and that we need to hear the Good News of God's love.

CHAPTER 2

1. Because all are sinners, and a *good* sinner is still a sinner, page 24.
2. God will judge them because they will not do what they know is right, v.1.
3. No one has ever lived a perfectly sinless life.
4. Glory - 16 times; Peace - 11 times; Law - 75 times. This shows that these words are very important.
5. They have their conscience, v.15.
6. He knew he was guilty and tried to make an excuse for what he had done, page 26.
7. Because God had given them His law, vs.17, 18, and they thought they could teach others, vs.19, 20.
8. He asked the Jews if they really kept God's law, vs.21-23.
9. He said they made God's house into a den of thieves. They were just as bad as "robbers of temples", page 27.
10. The Jews tried to tell Christians they must be circumcised, but this is not a command of God.
11. The Gentile who obeys, vs.25, 26.
12. Circumcision was a sign that a man was under God's covenant, and baptism is a sign that a Christian belongs to the Lord. Neither circumcision nor baptism can save anyone.

CHAPTER 3

1. The Jews had the great revelation from God, the Old Testament, v.2.
2. God the Creator, sets the standards of what is right for the whole universe, and anyone who opposes God must be wrong, v.4.
3. God never wants us to commit sin. He always has a better way to bring about what is really good, v.8.
4. There has never been a perfect man who committed no sin except the Lord Jesus Christ.
5. No excuse will help him, for all men are guilty.
6. Yes. That one sin makes him a sinner, and keeping the law cannot make him righteous, v.20. Also it is impossible for anyone to live without sinning.
7. God cannot set aside His own righteousness, but Christ died and paid the penalty, and so the sinner is free.
8. The grace of God led Him to give His Son; He has loved us with an eternal love, Jeremiah 31.3. So grace came first.
9. The Son of God paid the price and bought us for Himself.
10. The blood on the mercy seat speaks of the death of Christ, which means that God can show mercy and forgive us.
11. There is no difference, for all have sinned and all can be saved only through Christ.

CHAPTER 4

1. Abraham was justified by faith, not by works, so he could not boast, v.2.
2. You earn wages by working, but a gift is free, v.4.
3. Abraham and David did and perhaps many others.
4. When God justifies a man, He puts him on different ground before Him and will never call him guilty again. Justification is forever, but a man needs to be forgiven many times.
5. No, he is in God's family and the Father will teach him to obey.
6. He was justified long before he was circumcised, therefore no one can think that he was justified because he had been circumcised.
7. All Jews are the natural children of Abraham and all believers are the spiritual children of Abraham. This is because Abraham believed in God and those who believe are like him.
8. The almighty Creator can make anything exist, just by saying the word, page 44.
9. No; Abraham had wonderful faith in God's promises, but once he asked God to bless *Ishmael* because he could not believe that Sarah would have a son.
10. There are many reasons, but here Paul said it was so God could count us as righteous and show that we are right with Him.

CHAPTER 5

1. We have *peace* with God, v.1; we can enter into the *grace* of God, v.2, Our *hope* is in God, v.2, and we have the *love* of God, v.5. We will be *saved* from the wrath of God, v.9. We are now *friends* of God, v.10, and our *joy* is in God, v.11.
2. The last blessing is the greatest, because we have more joy in God the Giver than in all His gifts.
3. We know God loves us and allows trouble to come on us so we will become more like the Lord Jesus Christ. This makes us happy.
4. His Word tells us that we are already justified, by the blood of Christ, v.9.
5. He has shown us that He loves us and has *reconciled* us to Himself, vs.10, 11.
6. The Jews wanted to go back to Moses, but Paul showed that the Lord Jesus Christ is far greater than Adam, page 49.
7. Because they have the same nature as Adam, page 49.
8. He was the head of a race, and through one act he had a great effect on millions of people, page 49.
9. Adam's great action was disobeying God and this brought great trouble on all men. Christ obeyed God and so all men can be saved, pages 49,50.
10. Because all men have the nature of Adam and want to do just what God tells them not to do, v.20.

CHAPTER 6

1. The third one, that God will not judge him again as a sinner. For example, 3.24; 4.5; 5.1.
2. Romans 6, *sin;* Romans 7, *law;* Romans 8, *flesh.* See page 53.
3. We were dead in sin; now we are dead to sin.
4. By baptism, 6.4.
5. No, God will judge all men.
6. When He took our sins on Himself, page 54.
7. We should count ourselves as dead and risen with Christ, 6.11.
8. No part. God has bought us and we are altogether His.
9. Yes, a slave of God, but not of sin, 6.18,22.
10. No, they must die for their sins, 6.23.
11. Because no one can become a true son by his works, page 57.

CHAPTER 7

1. The law has a claim on a person as long as he lives, but not after he has died, v.1. For example, a woman cannot marry another man until her husband is dead.

2. A Christian is not bound to keep the law because he has died with Christ, vs.4, 6.
3. We can bring others to the Lord, pages 59,60.
4. Not by trying hard to keep the law, but in the power of the Holy Spirit, page 60.
5. I was born with a sinful nature, so when God tells me to do something, I want to do the opposite. I sin and therefore I have to die, v.10.
6. Natural death means that the body is separated from the soul. Spiritual death means that a man is separated from God, page 61.
7. The law is good because it shows me that sin is terrible in God's sight, v.13.
8. The law is good, but I am weak, vs.16-18.
9. Yes, before he learned that Christ could give the victory. But we all have the same nature so that these things are true of us also, page 64.
10. No, there is nothing good in the flesh, v.18. The Bible tells us we are dead in Christ, and can live a new life in Him because He will give us the victory, v.25.

CHAPTER 8

1. Not by baptism, or joining a church, but by receiving Christ, and asking Him to receive you, page 65.
2. He is God, and He gives us new life when we receive Christ, page 66; John 6.63.
3. It is not a new set of commands for the Christian to obey, but it is the general principle that the Spirit gives life to those who believe, page 66.
4. 1. The Lord Jesus perfectly fulfilled the law. 2. The law said sinners must die, but the Lord Jesus became responsible for our sins and died for them. 3. We can walk according to the Spirit, and so fulfil the righteous demands of the law, v.4.
5. We get new life when Christ comes into our hearts, and we get new bodies when He comes back again for us, page 68.
6. Yes, God's love to us is not like the world's love. God has given everything to Christ, and Christ will share all He has with us. But there will be special rewards for those who suffer with Christ, v.17.
7. The results of men's sin will be removed, page 70.
8. We were saved by faith, and we hope that God will take us to heaven some day and we are sure He will keep His word, v.24.
9. The Holy Spirit, v.27, and the Lord Jesus Christ, v.34.
10. His great purpose is to glorify His Son, the Lord Jesus Christ.
11. He can make me more like His Son, page 72.
12. Nothing can stop God from loving me, but sin can keep me from enjoying His love, page 74.

CHAPTER 9

1. No. He knew that every man must stand before God and only the Perfect Man could take on Himself the guilt of others.
2. Also see page 78.
3. He is a Man, a descendant of Israel. He is also the Supreme God, page 78.
4. The natural descendants of Abraham will have Abraham's spiritual blessings, if they have faith as Abraham did. All believers have faith, and they are the true spiritual descendants of Abraham, page 79.
5. God loves all men, but He loved Jacob more than Esau because Jacob wanted spiritual blessing. God chose Jacob before he was born; this was to show His grace, page 80.
6. God offers His mercy to all men, and no one will have any excuse; no one will be able to accuse God of being unfair, page 81.
7. Of course. God spoke to him many times through Moses. Pharaoh did not believe and he made his own heart harder. God knew in advance what would happen, but He did not force Pharaoh to disobey Him, page 82.
8. He is giving men more time to think, and to turn from their sins. He is also preparing us for heaven, and this takes time, v.23.
9. His beloved, 1.7; and His sons, 8.14, page 83.
10. They were no better than the men of Sodom and Gomorrah, except a few people who trusted in the Lord, v.29.
11. He is the Almighty God, and the Lord of all angels, page 84.
12. Because He never changes, and we can trust Him fully, page 85.

CHAPTER 10

1. Yes, but they did not know that God is so righteous He cannot accept good works in payment for sin, v.2.
2. (1) He fulfilled the law by obeying every command. (2) He accepted the penalty of the law when He died for sins, v.4. God has brought the old age of law to an end; since Christ died, it is the age of Grace.
3. Neither. God has brought His message to us, and commanded us to take it to others, vs.6-8.
4. When I accept Christ as my Saviour, I also accept Him as my Lord. If this is real, other people must know about it, so I confess with my lips that Jesus is my Lord. If I don't, I would go on in my old habits so I would not be saved from the **power** of sin, page 87.
5. Verse 10 is the order of events in my life: I believe and so I tell others. Verse 9 gives the order of events in Christ's experience: He always was Lord, but He became man, and rose from death, page 87.
6. God did both of these when I believed. But He justified me once, and this can never change. He saved me also once from the penalty of my

sins, and this will never be repeated, but He also keeps on saving me from the power of my old sinful habits every day until the Lord comes, p.88.

7. Isaiah 28.16: Romans 9.33 and 10.11. Joel 2.32: Acts 5.21, Romans 10.13. Isaiah 53.1: John 12.38 and Romans 10.16.

8. Tell them the Good News, v.17.

9. Through the world of nature which He created, v.18.

10. They loved other gods, and so He showed His love to other nations.

11. He did not really love these people; they had been the enemies of Israel many years.

CHAPTER 11

1. No; see 9.27. But the Holy Spirit led him to use very strong language, 10.21.

2. There were 7000 who did not worship idols, but they did not tell Elijah that they believed, vs.3,4. Perhaps they were afraid of Jezebel.

3. Because they were really the enemies of God, pages 93,94.

4. Psalm 23.5; Matthew 22.4; Revelation 3.20.

5. No, God will not save anyone who does not want Him, or who rejects the Lord Jesus Christ. Many Jews will believe in the Lord during the years of the Great Tribulation and others will die before Christ comes again. So all the people of Israel who are still alive will be saved, Zechariah 12.10.

6. Israel has rejected God's Son, so God is sending the Good News to Gentiles, and this is a great blessing for those who believe, v.12.

7. All Israel belongs to God, but only those who believe will be saved.

8. No, it is all God's grace and every branch gets its blessing from the root, page 96.

9. No, but still He will not save people who reject His beloved Son.

10. Individual Jews are being saved today and the nation will be saved when the Lord comes, page 96.

11. No; any living man can accept God's mercy, but in the future many Jews will turn to Him.

12. Because the Father chose to reveal Himself to unlearned people.

CHAPTER 12

1. The first two verses tell us to do God's will and this is more important than anything else, page 102.

2. God has bought us for Himself and we should offer ourselves to Him, our bodies, all that we are, verse 1.

3. So they can help one another in the assembly, page 102.

4. There are no true prophets who can tell what will happen next, but God has told us from Scripture about the great events of the future, page 103.

5. I should go to him and try to help him. Real love does not mean that I should let him go on in sin.
6. We are the Lord's servants and want others to know Him, page 105.
7. The Holy Spirit will help me act like Christ, page 106.
8. They will soon have quarrels and start fighting, page 106.

CHAPTER 13

1. In some countries people elect their own government; and in others the army helps a few men to take power. But the Bible teaches that Christians should obey the government and not fight against it, vs.1,2.
2. The government has the authority to punish me if I do not obey; and my conscience will also trouble me, v.5.
3. No one likes to pay taxes, but the Christian should honestly pay all his taxes, vs.6,7.
4. You should love your neighbour as yourself, v.9, but it is still more important to love your God with everything you are and have, Matthew 22.37,38.
5. The Holy Spirit has told us some of the things which will happen when the Lord comes and these things are beginning to happen today, page 110.
6. The world, the flesh and the devil, page 110.
7. We are not told to fight against the flesh. We should not think about what our old nature wants or try to please it, 8.6-13; 13.14.

CHAPTER 14

1. They do not understand that they have been set free from the law and they think they should obey rules about food and sabbath days, vs.2,5.
2. His own Master is able to keep him from doing wrong, and will judge him if he does wrong, v.4.
3. He knows they **all** belong to God, pages 112,113.
4. We are saved by faith and we must not let anyone tell us we can be saved by keeping the law, page 113.
5. Believers will receive rewards for serving the Lord. Believers who live for their own pleasure will lose their reward but not their eternal life, page 114.
6. In small matters we should not judge one another, but we cannot let a brother or sister keep on committing sin.

CHAPTER 15

1. No, He tried to help men, but always did what His Father wanted.
2. Yes, if it is for God's glory. We should not receive those who are teaching what is not true or who are living in sin or who will cause trouble in the church.
3. To fulfil God's promises to Israel and to bring great blessing to the Gentiles.
4. Paul quoted four verses from the Old Testament in Romans 15.9-12.
5. Christ the Son of God is the Creator of all men, but as a Man He is a descendant of Jesse, page 118.
6. Many Gentiles believed in the Lord when Paul preached the good news to them, pages 119, 120.
7. No, only the Holy Spirit can do this, page 120.
8. He was busy preaching the Good News to people who had not heard about Christ. Now he wanted to stop at Rome on his way to Spain.
9. (1) That God would keep him safe at Jerusalem, v.31.
   (2) That the Christians there would accept the money he brought, v.31.
   (3) That he might be able to visit the believers in Rome, v.32.
10. Yes, but Paul was arrested and did not reach Rome until four years later, still a prisoner.

CHAPTER 16

1. She was a Christian woman who had helped him and many others also, and she would be glad to have some friends in the big city.
2. Paul loved all the Lord's people, but perhaps especially the first man whom he had won for Christ in Asia. We can be sure Epaenetus loved Paul for bringing him to the Lord.
3. Paul spoke of Rufus' mother as if she were his own mother, but this meant that she had been very kind to Paul.
4. He may be a very good talker, but every Christian should understand God's Word, so that he will know when someone is trying to teach what is not true.
5. Grace and peace, page 127.
6. Christ will give honour to those who have served Him faithfully and we will praise God for ever, v.27; page 128.
7. That we should give the Good News to men of all nations.